HINDU-BUDDHIST PHILOSOPHY
on
CONFLICT AVOIDANCE
and
ENVIRONMENT CONSCIOUSNESS

Hindu-Buddhist Philosophy *on* Conflict Avoidance *and* Environment Consciousness

SAMVAD—A GLOBAL INITIATIVE (III)

Vivekananda International Foundation
New Delhi

PENTAGON PRESS LLP

First published in 2025 by
PENTAGON PRESS LLP
206, Peacock Lane, Shahpur Jat
New Delhi-110049, India
Contact: 011-26490600

Typeset in Adobe Garamond, 11 Point
Printed at Thomson Press (I) LTD

ISBN 978-93-90095-92-6 (HB)

www.pentagonpress.in

CONTENTS

INTRODUCTION

SAMVAD-III

Global Hindu-Buddhist Initiative for Conflict Avoidance – Inter-Religious Understanding and Interdependent Sustainability

Ulaanbaatar, Mongolia
September 6 and 7, 2019

The III Edition of Samvad at Ulaanbaatar was a great success in many ways. In particular, it cemented the relation between India and Mongolia as Spiritual Partners. It was held in the premises of Gandan Monastery in Ulaanbaatar.

The pre-inaugural session was dominated by the Buddhist spirit at its best, with a large crowd of a couple of hundreds attending the rituals and opening of the gates of the new Gandan Monastery. The atmosphere was festive, with colourful traditional arts and music on display. The music and dance bore a lot of resemblance to that of NE India. UNICEF Goodwill Ambassador from Nepal, a Buddhist Nun, sang the Ganesh Stuti. Buddhist Spiritual Masters, Scholars, Policy Influencers from Sri Lanka, Bhutan, Nepal, Myanmar, Vietnam, Russia, Cambodia, Thailand, South Korea, Hong Kong and Japan participated in Samvad III along with the Mongolian and the Indian side.

The Prime Minister of Mongolia represented the Mongolian side. The entire proceedings had the blessings of His Eminence Khamba Lama, the Supreme Monk of Gandan Monastery.

Prime Minister of India, Mr Narendra Modi, gave a special video message for the occasion.

Mr S Gurumurthy, Chairman of the VIF and Ku Nivedita Bhide, one of its trustees, led the Indian delegation. Mr Sushil Modi, Deputy Chief Minister of Bihar, Dr Vinay Sahasrabuddhe, Member of Parliament (Rajya Sabha) & President, ICCR and Ladakh MP Mr Jamyang Tsering Namgyal were special nominees of the Prime Minister of India. Three eminent Indian religious and spiritual masters participated in the three-day proceedings: Sri Sri Ravi Shankar, Pujya Sri Avedshananada Giri ji and Pujya Sri Mitrananda.

Dr Swapan Dasgupta, MP; Balbir Punj, Former MP; and Dr Anirban Ganguly, Director-SPMRF, spoke at various sessions and interacted with Mongolian academia, civil society representatives, and students.

The VIF organising team was headed by its Secretary Smt Anuttama Ganguly.

From the Japanese side, in addition to the Shinto-Buddhist religious scholars, academicians, and Japanese Foundation officials, the Ambassador of Japan to Mongolia participated and read PM Abe's message.

Samvad III was divided into two parts: a round table of Religious and Spiritual Masters and a parallel session on the aspects of Conflict Avoidance, Shared Values, Democracy, *and Environmental Consciousness.*

Religious Round Table [RRT]

The RRT is a path-breaking exercise introduced to carry forward the theme of Conflict Avoidance articulated in the concept paper of Samvad, which Shri S Gurumurthy delivered as the keynote speech at Samvad I in 2015 in New Delhi.

The concept paper had alluded to the Hindu-Buddhist traditional dialogue model of *Tarka Shastra* and *Purva Paksha* among scholars to question the premises and foundations of the other faiths to seek clarity and to avoid conflicts that arise because of the miscommunication and misinterpretation by religious scholars themselves. The Hindu-Buddhist model is different and is termed as inter-faith dialogue. It is an open and frank expression of misgivings of one faith about the other so as to remove the misgivings and to ensure no one in any way spreads violent ideas as legitimate theological positions of a religion. The Hindu-Buddhist dialogues had effectively prevented any mass religious or other killings in India till the 13th century.

The Indian way of dialogue effectively avoids conflicts and ensures that religions grow as philosophical religions that are willing to engage in dialogue over their foundations and not as ideological religions that do not. Swami Vivekananda had indirectly introduced the *Purva Paksha* model in the **World Parliament of Religions** and directly in his talks thereafter. But for a whole century, the world dismissed religion as a factor and the need for dialogue among them for peace and harmony till the 1990s when two conflicting views of the end of conflicts, as Francis Fukuyama theorised, or the re-beginning of religious conflicts, as Samuel Huntington hypothesised, emerged. It was then that Harvard University thought it fit to commence the Religious Pluralism Project, recalling the 1893 World Parliament of Religions.

Yet there has been no effort for open discussions on the foundations of different faiths, which affect the relation between faiths and, therefore, between peoples. This is despite the fact that a wealth of literature on religious fundamentalism and extremism had emerged through the ***Fundamentalism Project*** of the American Academy of Arts and Science [Chicago University Press] in the late 1980s and early 1990s. Simultaneously, Hans Kung, a well-known Catholic theologian, formulated a rule for inter-religious dialogue that is identical to the Hindu-Buddhist concept of Tarka Shastra and Purva Paksha. Hans Kung formulated: "*No peace among the nations without peace among the religions; No peace among the religions without dialogue between the religions; No dialogue between the religions, without investigation of the foundations of the religions.*"

The concept paper of Samvad I is founded on the Hindu Buddhist dialogue discipline of Tarka and Purva Paksha as formulated by Hans Kung. It was in Samvad II that the VIF thought it would be necessary to start an honest and open dialogue among faiths. In Samvad II, besides Hindu Buddhist spiritual masters, Muslims and Christian religious leaders also participated. They could openly discuss the concept and terminology of one faith, which could create apprehensions in the minds of the followers of other faiths. The leaders who participated in the discussions were enthused by the dialogue format. After the Myanmar dialogue, there was also a follow-up dialogue in India. This dialogue was conducted and moderated by Swami Mitrananda of Chinmaya Mission.

The Ulaanbaatar Samvad III took the concept to another level. Issues relating to what is the concept of Kafir, Jihad, Heathen, Crusade, and Conversions were discussed in detail. The discussions touched upon the need for faiths to move away from ***Only* to *Also***, and ***Conversion* to *Conversation*.** One of the important effects of the RRT in Myanmar was the message of Daw Aung San Sui Kyi, the State Counsellor of The Republic of the Union of Myanmar to the Ulaanbaatar meet where she specifically said:

> "*[S]ome of the responsible religionists do not take interest in imparting knowledge of the genuine knowledge of the genuine teachings shown by their*

respective religions. Moreover, some even lead their followers the wrong way by means of instructing them bogus and insincere doctrines under the name of religion."

Technical session on Conflict Avoidance, Shared Values, Democracy and Environmental Consciousness

The parallel technical sessions, the mainstay of the conference, with the themes of Shared Values, Democracy, environmental Consciousness, and Conflict Avoidance, saw participation by a large number of spiritual masters and academics, thinkers, policy makers, and leaders.

The parallel sessions on both days had interesting themes, themes which essentially defined the deliberations and the sharing of views and experiences in *Samvad.* One session had as its theme, 'Conflict Avoidance" and "Shared Values and Democracy in Asia", while the other session had "Environment Consciousness" and "Conflict Avoidance." These sessions saw as speakers members of Parliament from India, Sri Lanka and Mongolia, officials from various agencies and bodies of the United Nations such as UNDP and UNICEF, scholars from Bhutan, from Harvard University, from South Korea, from the National University of Mongolia, the nodal social science research body in Mongolia Academy of Sciences. On day two, the environment and tourism Minister of Mongolia, Mr N Tserenbat delivered a special address and spoke on the "The Green Passport Campaign", a very interesting and unique initiative in Mongolia to spread environmental consciousness, awareness, responsibility and sensitivity among citizens and especially the youth and children.

Several ideas and themes were discussed: the vision of shared values, leadership, governance and environmental conservation in Asia, the increasing and perennial relevance of Swami Vivekananda's message, especially in the context of conflict avoidance, the articulation of a narrative of a free and open Indo-Pacific, the need to address environmental challenges, challenges emanating from terrorism, from an increasing imbalance in our collective existence, the need for a new geo-strategic and cultural vision for the region, the 21st century being the Asian century with Buddha's message being one of its defining cores and many such themes were discussed and deliberated upon. The transformative governance initiatives in India, their origin from the philosophy of compassion – *Karuna*, Prime Minister Modi's efforts to transform India – through inclusion and empowerment, through peoples' power and participation, the Indian approach to environmental consciousness, the works of Mongolian monks in environmental conservation were some of the topics that the speaker's focused on.

The idea that along with rights, citizens globally need to be made aware of the concept of duties – that along with *Lokatantra – democracy*, there needed to be *Lokakartavya – duty* towards one's society, milieu, people and country also came up in the discussions. The views that there can be no hegemony in terms of the flow of ideas, freedom of following one's ways of life and worship and that Asia and the eastern wisdom – flowing from Buddhist and Hindu philosophies and traditions – *paramparas* – was emphasised and discussed. The perception was also that sharing experience in governance and environmental initiatives was essential for evolving and articulating a new narrative of engagement.

At the end of the two-day deliberations in Ulaanbaatar, a Declaration was made which captured the essence of the discussions at RRT and RTEC.

S. Gurumurthy
Chairman, VIF

1

Narendra Modi

"Samvad celebrates the ancient Asian philosophic values which are best represented in the Hindu-Buddhist civilisational streams; these values also serve as a guiding light to those ideologies that thrive on conflicts and hate. At the same time, this forum will also throw light on mitigating human conflicts with environment, which is facing great strain today."

– **Narendra Modi**
Prime Minister of India

Namaste,

Dear Friends, I am delighted that the third edition of Samvad is taking place; the word Samvad means dialogue. This forum is a shared desire between my good friend, Japanese PM Shinzo Abe, and me. The aim is to promote people to people interactions that lead to conflict avoidance and environmental consciousness. I compliment the various individuals and Think-Tanks who have initiated Samvad and made it grow. I am happy that this edition of Samvad is taking place in Ulaanbaatar in Mongolia.

We in India consider Mongolia to be our spiritual friend, spiritual brother. The light of Buddhism started to shine in Mongolia centuries ago, thanks to monks who went there, mainly from India. The distance or climate did not deter the spirit of these great monks. They became the earliest binding force between India and Mongolia.

India-Mongolia friendship got a huge boost through the work of Kushok Bakula Rinpoche, who was India's Ambassador in Mongolia from 1990 to 2000. Inspired by Lord Buddha, he lived not for himself but for others. His numerous community service efforts touched lives across the world and particularly in India and Mongolia.

Narendra Modi, Prime Minister of India.

The Pethub monastery, that he established, will be an enduring symbol of our links. In May last year, I had travelled to Leh where I had joined the birth Centenary celebration of the Great Kushok Bakula Rinpoche, and earlier this year, I was again in Leh to lay the foundation of a modern airport which is named after Kushok Bakula Rinpoche.

Distinguished guests, I vividly remember my visit to Mongolia in 2015, the first Prime Ministerial visit to this beautiful nation. During that visit, I had the honour of addressing the Mongolian parliament; I can never forget my visit to the Gandan Monastery, where I had presented a Bodhi tree sapling to the Venerable Hamba Lama.

I am told that a Buddha statue at the Gandan Monastery will be unveiled soon; this is one more symbol of our shared heritage.

Friends, Saṃvad celebrates the ancient Asian philosophic values which are best represented in the Hindu-Buddhist civilisational streams; these values also serve as a guiding light to those ideologies that thrive on conflicts and hate. After all, conflict avoidance and openness are at the core of Hinduism and Buddhism. At the same time, this forum will also throw light on mitigating human conflicts with environment, which is facing great strain today.

Distinguished guests, while I am addressing these distinguished gathering, it is natural to recall the noble teachings of Lord Buddha which remain one of the greatest unifying forces in world the history. He not only brought people closer but also further unity among societies that were in conflict with each other. Imagine, the moral courage he had to walk-up to one of the most dreaded dacoits of that time – Aṅgulimāla and win him over just with a power of compassion and love. He was blessed with the power to go right in the midst of conflict and bring peace. Who can forget the manner in which he ensured peace between the Sakyas and the Koliyas. When Lord Buddha learned that these people were at war with each other, he was deeply anguished. He decided to go to these people and find the root cause of the conflict. When he asked why they were fighting, he got no clear answer for a long time. Eventually, he discovered that the fight was due to very little water. Lord Buddha wanted to know if there was indeed so much water to cause such bitter conflicts. More so, when so many lives were at the stake, the resounding answer was no. Lord Buddha asked the warring people to introspect on their deeds, considering that for a handful of water, so much blood would have flown; he also called for leading a life free from conflict. His powerful words were enough to bring both – peace and sanity among those fighting.

Distinguished guests, Lord Buddha did not approve of dividing society into fragments. He ensured that the principles of Buddhism were very clear in their rejection of violence and mindless hate; at the same time, he did not stop at just rejection; he also emphasised on serving society and eliminating every form of human suffering. After all, a world free from suffering would also mean a world free from conflicts.

Friends, today, my mind also goes back to another September, the September of 1893, when a saint from India beautifully articulated our contribution to conflict avoidance; yes, I am talking about Swami Vivekananda and his address at the world parliament of religions in Chicago. He did not agree with the conventional virtue of merely tolerating another faith because that implied that one faith is inferior to another. He spoke about acceptance which is steps ahead of mere tolerance. Swami Vivekananda advocated dialogue as a conflict avoidance model for differing faiths; the spirit of dialogue is not exclusive. It has ample space for other, often differing points of view. The moment we begin accepting the points of others and provide that space for debate as well as discussion, room for conflict disappears.

Friends, I am proud to belong to India that considers the world as our family. When we believe in this principle, we cannot even think about conflict, but in a time when parochial ideologies are on the rise, our cultural source, the way in balancing both the national interest and global wellbeing. For this, we take inspiration from Mahatma Gandhi who said, and I quote "It is impossible for one to be internationalist without being a nationalist. Internationalism is possible only when nationalism becomes a fact that is when people belong to different countries have organized themselves and are able to act as one man." The wise Bapu cautioned societies seeking to profit at the cost of the other and dreamt of an India that would work for humanity at large. 21st-century India is doing precisely that. We are catering the national challenges along with a strong emphasis on making our world better. We see this spirit when India takes the lead with France in creating the international solar alliance to harness the rays of the sun for a better tomorrow. We see this spirit when the tiger population in India doubles in a span of 10 years-improving the balance of nature. We see this spirit, when India is working towards eliminating single-use plastic; we also see the spirit in the efforts of ensuring proper usage of water resources. India's success in this not only will touch the lives of 130 crore Indians but will also help other nations of the world.

Distinguished guests, care for the environment is also at the core of our vision of *Vasudhaiva Kutumbakam*. We are taught that nature is our own extension, and that is why we will take care of it in good times and bad.

Friends, let us create a world free from mindless hate, violence, bloodshed where we are all able to live together happily. Yes, there will be diversities and differences, but diversity is nothing but the plan of Mother Nature. It is Mother Nature who is manifesting herself in the form of these diversities; when we understand this diversity and accept this beauty, we will also understand that differences do not mean opposition. That is when urge for conflict will automatically drop. Homogeneity is not only undesirable but also boring. Our diversity strengthens us and make us vibrant and intellectually richer. May we celebrate this diversity, learn from each other and leave behind a better planet for our future generations.

Friends, I understand that a religious roundtable of all major world religions, intellectuals, and thinkers will be held parallelly as part of Samvad. This is a great effort. I wish the Samvad meet and the religious roundtable all success.

Thank you all, thank you very much, Namaste.

2

SHINZO ABE

"Among all human virtues, 'mercy' is the most fundamental. Buddhism teaches the importance of this 'mercy' from the very beginning."

– Shinzo Abe
Former Prime Minister of Japan

Hello everyone. I'm Shinzo Abe. I heartily welcome that the third "SAMVAD" is held in Ulaanbaatar.

This is the 5th seminar since it started in 2015 based on the joint proposal of Prime Minister Modi and myself. I would like to congratulate that this conference is held in Mongolia which shares universal values with Japan.

Among all kind of human virtues, "mercy" is said to be the most fundamental in various religions. Buddhism teaches the importance of the mind of this "mercy" from the outset.

In Shinto, the indigenous faith in Japan, there is a phrase "In the sight of mercy, nothing is to be hated". It is not easy for human beings to attain that state of mind overnight, but that is where we want to reach.

These ways of thinking have shaped the "tolerance" that is the origin of Asian values, and have supported the "diversity" in Asia.

This year marks the 150th birth anniversary of Gandhi. During my visit to India in 2017, Prime Minister Modi showed me around Sabarmati Ashram, the ancient residence of Mahatma Gandhi. Gandhi is known for his tolerance for other religions.

Based on the traditions of "tolerance" and "diversity", values such as "freedom" and "democracy" have blossomed in Asia. Today, these traditions

---

Shinzo Abe, Former Prime Minister of Japan.

and values in Asia are spreading as a foundation of a free and open order that will bring stability and prosperity to all countries without discrimination.

On the other hand, the spirit of "tolerance" in Asian tradition is now facing a threat. Violent extremism in the name of religion has led to an increasing number of attempts to deny others and to paint the world with violence.

Using the analogy of a raft Buddha once preached.

"It is foolish to carry a raft, which is useful for crossing a river, on one's shoulder even after one has crossed the river in the belief that 'it is a precious thing'."

If one cherished the doctrine of religion resulting in conflict with the people, it would rather undermine the essence. This is my understanding of the teaching of Buddha.

In May this year, Japan opened a new era of "Reiwa". "Wa" means "Respecting and helping each other".

Since the time of Prince Shotoku in the 6th century, Japan has nurtured the sense of values that "Harmony is the greatest of virtues". We hope, in the era of "Reiwa" too, that Japan and the world respect "Wa" or harmony. I wish today's discussion will lead to the realization of such a world.

Thank you for your attention.

3

Aung San Suu Kyi

"The survival of humankind depends on our ability to return to the genuine teachings of our faiths and to live in harmony with each other and with nature."

-

– **Aung San Suu Kyi**
Former State Counsellor of Myanmar

- The most Venerables and Your Holiness,
- Excellencies, Distinguished Participants,
- Eminent Scholars and Spiritual Leaders, – Ladies and Gentlemen!

It is a great pleasure and honour for me to convey my sincere greetings and heartfelt congratulations through video message to the Samvad III, which is jointly organized by the Vivekananda International Foundation (VIF, New Delhi) and Gaudan Thegchenling Monastery – Centre of Mongolian Buddhists in association with the International Buddhist Confederation (IBC), Asian Buddhist Conference for Peace (ABCP), the Japan Foundation and Institute of Strategic Studies, Mongolia. It also gives me a great pleasure and honour to extend my warm greetings and best wishes to all of the esteemed participants from different faiths of various countries and organizations for taking part in this august assembly.

Every religion teaches us the best of all the best in the world by two parallel ways – showing the good and ethical way of life, teaching or theory and putting the theory into practice – empirical application. Most of religious followers and leaders discharged these two duties and thus civilized and cultured human

Aung San Suu Kyi, Former State Counsellor of the Republic of the Union of Myanmar, and the Union Minister for Foreign Affairs of Myanmar Government.

societies manifested themselves on the surface of the globe. Responsible religious leaders were also able to lead their followers to virtuous and righteous ways of living. As a consequence, most parts of the globe were the pleasant and peaceful habitats to live in.

But in later times along with through the technology of modern civilization, modern populace have to face a great deal of predicament – a big gap in modern life between profession and practice. The religious faith they have already confessed may be of immense help to them but they neglect their religious teachings without going to their religious centres. Simultaneously some of the responsible religionists do not take interest in imparting knowledge of the genuine knowledge of the genuine teachings shown by their respective religions. Moreover, some even lead their followers to the wrong way by means of instructing then bogus and insincere doctrines under the name of religion. Staying along from religious teachings and disbelieving in them the population of atheists, heathens, agnostics, pagans, infidels, boors, vulgarians and barbarians become greater and greater in number than ever.

At present, we, all of the diverse religious leaders, have to make an arduous efforts to save this unwelcome situation and reform our approach to the sustainability of the faithful. First, we, all the religious leaders have to demonstrate convincingly to them that the genuine teachings and implementation and application of them have a profound and beneficial effects. And then we have to lead them to the fields of learning and practising, being equipped with the fundamental principles of moral ethics. All religious leaders in the world have to be builders of a peaceful and prosperous human society influenced by religious teachings and involve themselves in consolidating peace and security of the world. Besides, members of diverse religions have to build mutual understanding, respect and trust among each other in order to obtain a peaceful and prosperous human society, refraining from interfering in matters of other religions and cooperating for peace, and denouncing all kinds of hate-speech and false propaganda under the pretext of religion, and conflicts and wars resulted from such activities. We all have to strongly condemn all those who instigate religious conflicts by using various methods and those who provide support or involve themselves in such activities.

If we do not pay deep regard to the doctrinal teachings and the relevant empirical applications, the world we live in will unquestionably devasted by extremism or terrorism, the creation of infidels, boors, vulgarians and barbarians. The whole world has been unbalanced and unhinged by the said destructive and obstructive elements who are the major hindrances and obstructions to the construction of global peace and prosperity. Before these elements have become greater in numbers all of the religious leaders have to work together in unison and to endeavour without any fear and the slightest hesitation in order to obtain social life with full security assurances, including an inherent duty of all faiths to conserve the environment before it is too late to survive our humankind.

As paragons of virtue and righteousness by ourselves, let us lead our global followers to build a global peace and prosperity by teaching and showing good exemplary ways and means.

May I take this opportunity to convey my best wishes and respectful greetings to all the participants for the great success of this auspicious conference with the Supreme Virtues of the Buddha.

May all the religious teachers and leaders be united and happy in order to tread on the same common platform!

Thank you.

4

S. GURUMURTHY

"*The Samvad initiative reminds us that environmental consciousness is not just a policy but a spiritual responsibility, a call to live in harmony with the Earth.*"

– S. Gurumurthy

Namaskarams to all!

When we discuss the subject of environmental consciousness, we are discussing a paradigm difference. The current discourse is centred on environmental regulation. The laws that the government passes and also the environmental conventions, which are intergovernmental conventions, all constitute regulations.

Here in Samvad, we are not talking about regulations at all; we are not talking about governments. We are talking about age-old philosophies of life and lifestyle and how that philosophy and lifestyle had protected the environment for thousands of years, and how new ideologies and new ways of life, which have disturbed the relationship between humans and nature, is what we have to discuss.

All philosophies and ideologies are finally rooted in religions that define man's relation with the creation, which is nature. Coming to religions, there are, among religions, two different paradigms of religion. One set of religions says that the entire world is a manifestation of God and human beings are integral; human beings are not independent of creation; they are part of creation. They are as important as man has to live together with whether it is trees, rivers, or animals. This is one paradigm. Another paradigm is that God created man in his own image and created the world for man's consumption.

S. Gurumurthy, Chairman, Vivekananda International Foundation, India.

These are two different paradigms, and there has been a huge debate right from the days of Lynn White, who wrote an article in Science magazine in the year 1965 where he brought about this distinction that the religions that consider the creation as intended for the consumption of human beings have been responsible for environmental destruction.

There is a need to consider how these two paradigms operate. I will tell you how these four religious streams, the Indic religious streams, consider the relationship between nature and humans sacred. The other religions consider the relationship secular. This is the difference.

The four religions are the Hindu, Buddha, Jain and Sikh religions. What do they talk about nature and the relationship between nature and humans? The most critical text of the Hindus is the Ishavasya Upanishad; of course, you can find it in many other texts also. Ishavasya Upanishad says, "*Isavasyamidam sarvam*", i.e., "The Lord manifested as everything in this world". Mahatma Gandhi translated this as meaning, "Everything down to the tiniest atom is divine." In fact, Mahatma Gandhi went to the extent of saying, "If all the Hindu literature is destroyed and only this one sentence remains, that will be sufficient to make the Hindus rise again." That is the extent of importance that he gave to this one sentence.

So, in the philosophy of Isavasya Upanishad, everything is a manifestation of God. You cannot say that this is something intended for me; no, you are also intended for that. And then in Kalachakra Tantra, Buddhism says the same thing, except that Buddhism does not recognise the concept of Brahman. But it recognises the concept of vacuum, emptiness, the undefined, unrecognised, incomprehensible force. But Shankara described that Vacuum as Brahman – "That which you say as Vacuum is what I call Brahman." That is why, in the debates in India, Shankara is known to be Buddha in concealed form; he said what Buddha said but in a mirror form. So what Kalachakra Tantra says is, "Earth, Water, Fire, Air and Humans all emerged from the same Vacuum." It is not that vacuum created nature for the enjoyment of man., So far as the relationship between man and nature is concerned, there is, in substance, no difference between Hinduism and Buddhism. Both view the relationship between the Panch Buthas and the humans identically.

And then take the Jains. The Jain text, Acharya Mahavira's Sutra Texts, says, "That all Panch Buthas – Earth, Water, Fire, Air and Space – are not lifeless matter; they have Atma, a soul." All of them are saying the same thing in different languages. Of course, if we look at the original language in which it is written, there may not be differences in words also.

The Sikh Guru Granth Sahib then says that the Panch Bhutas – Earth, Water, Fire, Space, and all Living Beings, including Man – emerged from the same Brahman.

These four faiths constitute one distinct paradigm.

The distinction between the Indic religious paradigm and other paradigm is brought out by Reverend Father Shaji Kochuthara an Indian Christiaan theologist. He did doctoral research on the theological difference between Abrahamic and Indic religions. He has explained the result of his study in a profound cross-philosophical paper titled "Rediscovering Christian Eco-Theological Ethics" which deals with the comparative philosophical positions of the West and India. He writes that the reverence for nature which Vedas and Upanishads expounds are absent in the Abrahamic faiths and he says that Christianity will have to develop reverence for nature.

The distinction between the Indic and Abrahamic faiths is important because faiths influence not just people's thinking but also their conduct. Here is my personal experience with what faith means to me.

My village, where I come from, has a custom not to cut a tree if there is a pregnant woman in the family. There is also a custom to get permission from the tree itself before it is cut! A letter seeking its permission is hung around it and waits for a week. If there is no bad news in that period, the tree is supposed to have given the okay to be cut! This happened in my own life. We had a two-ground plot, which was a 4,800 square feet plot, and we were a joint family, and we had to put up a construction in that. We needed every inch of that land for construction. There were three coconut trees. Cutting coconut trees is considered a sin. We sought permission from the coconut trees and then only cut them. And there was a Neem tree almost at the centre of the plot. The architect said it had to be cut; otherwise, we could not build a house for our large family. We all decided to never cut the tree to have more space. We reduced our space, by nearly 1200 square feet.

In our house, one can even see that the tree stands which the house surrounds on three sides. We could not have cut that tree and lived in that house. That is the spiritual relationship between us and the tree. This comes from a philosophy and a lifestyle that reveres trees. Every Friday, we worship that tree. This is because of the philosophical approach that has been ingrained in us.

I am not talking about philosophers; I am not talking about Shankaracharya and Buddha; I am talking about very ordinary people who may not know any script. The reverence for nature is integral to all ancient civilisations. You Google for Malshegu Grove in Ghana. The traditional people of Ghana worship the Malshegu Grove. They live with the trees and eat animals they live with. They know when to cut the tree, where, which tree is to be cut, and which animal is to be hunted even they live on that. They invade them only to the extent of their needs and keep them as natural capital for their future generations. They have a living and ongoing relationship with nature.

When there were attempts to make them give up their faith as animistic and when commercial interests lured them they began cutting the grove which they worshipped once. Ghana government had to stop those activities to protect the Malshegu Grove.

This is the paradigm difference between the two sets of religious beliefs. Reverend Father Shaji Kochuthara writes about this reverence for nature. Kuchuthara's essay is very long. I wish to read out the first paragraph: "Christianity is the theology of dominating the earth; it is often accused of having been responsible for the present crisis."

We all look at it as intellectuals and thinkers who know how to save the environment. It is wrong. Ordinary people show us the way by their reverential relation with nature. We have to understand how religion influences humans. Every human being is influenced by some faith. Ninety-nine per cent of the people in India believe in God, and 100 per cent of people believe in astrology. Human beings have faith as the centre of their being. All traditional faiths teach, and their adherents practice reverence for nature. This is absent in contemporary faiths.

And so Reverend Kochuthara says, "That certain emphasis in Christian tradition did not facilitate reverential attitude towards nature." This is sacredness; you consider nature as sacred. On the other hand, Kochuthara writes, Christianity says that "Uncompromising commitment to the transcendental God and prohibition of the worship of any other thing", – whether it is tree or animal – "is prohibited, implying denial of the eminence of God." He goes on to say – "Any attempt to consider nature as sacred would be labelled as idolatry, and the Christian emphasis on the spiritual nature of human beings over and against the physical nature of the other creatures are some of the main reasons for the lack of reverence for nature in the Christian tradition...."

Even though Kochuthara rightly says that “it is unjust to attribute to Christianity the sole responsibility of environmental destruction,” and there are other reasons, including industrial and commercial reasons.

But it is now fairly established that traditional faiths revere nature which modern faiths do not. It is that reverence which transforms into environmental consciousness. Environmental consciousness makes protecting environment an individual’s moral duty. The stronger the faith the more inviolable is the moral duty. We need to recall and rebuild that moral duty and to make environmental consciousness a people’s movement.

This essentially falls in the domain of the Hindu Buddhist civilisations which have preserved their reverential attitude to creation and nature. That was why when the Hindu Buddhist Samvad was conceptualised and initiated environmental consciousness became one of the pillars of the Samvad. Environment being the biggest challenge of humanity today undoubtedly a massive Hindu Buddhist civilisational thrust is needed to save environment by promoting reverence for nature and not just consider nature as just a secular asset.

5

AMRITH BHARGAV

Background

The thematic thrust on the subject of Conflict avoidance in the context of the interplay of its natural elements leads to the inevitable study of consciousness in the environmental sense. Dialectically, cosmic law is manifested as omnipresent through the environment and its natural character. Regarded as the watchkeeper of cyclical time, environmental consciousness sets Indian Philosophy into the depths of the contemporary currents in environmental protection and conservation. Post-Industrialised behaviour, based on trade values and principles of exchange, is centred on the commodification of culture. This approach was sharply contrasted with the Indian/Eastern model of integrated environmental engagement, which was predicated on co-existence, reverence and contentment. The basis of the global discourse on Environmental action arises from the divergence between Western Universalism and Eastern Universality. The former rests on *conquest, colonisation and consumption,*[1] while the latter draws on *connection, communication and consciousness.*[2] While the former perceives life to be hierarchical in some sense or the other, the latter theorises life to be a web of networks.[3] This paper seeks to explore the comparative mindset in achieving inter-elemental consciousness in environmental action.

The Sacred Environment: Aspects of Creation

Sacral domains, within and without, comprise the fundamental core of Hindu Religion as it is known even today. The environmental aspect of creation is a

Amrith Bhargav, Research Scholar, Shanmugha Arts, Science, Technology & Research Academy (SASTRA), India.

facet of this pervasive sacredness, inextricable from all life. Life is sacred. Energy is also sacred. This sacralised approach places environmental concerns at the level of consciousness, uniting them with the civilisation continuum. Further, this aspect of sacredness has found recognition across academic timelines. This was best stated in the following unflinching terms by Dr S Radhakrishnan (1948):

> "*a recognition of spiritual realities not by abstention from the world, but by bringing to its life, its business (artha) and its pleasure (kama), the controlling power of spiritual faith.* ***Life is one, and in it, there is no distinction of sacred and secular. Bhakti and Mukti are not opposed. Dharma, artha and kama go together.***"[4]

Further, this cultural element found exemplified treatment in this passage:

> "*How more profound is India's traditional world, where each stone is a hierophant, a sign of the presence of the sacred in our world? Every sunrise here becomes a cosmogenic drama, every woman an embodiment of the tantric principle of Shakti. Behind the exterior forms specific only of India hides the sublime universal paradigm of the traditional conscience totally opposite to the modernistic one, also far more vibrant and wholesome. The craving of human soul for sacral archetypes is unquenchable, and archetypes are easily juxtaposed with new-age constructs. The sacral and the profane coexist.*"[5]

With detailed reference to cultural practices amongst the indigenous Red Indians, whose religion and culture revered nature like ours, India's highest Court explained illustratively in ***Sachidanand Pandey v. The State of West Bengal (1987)*** by quoting the response of the Indian Chief in the United States:

> *"Every part of the earth is sacred to my people. Every shining pine needle, every sandy shore, every mist in the dark woods, every clearing and humming insect is holy in the memory and experience of my people. The Sap, which courses through the trees, carries the memories of the red man.*
>
> *So, when the Great Chief in Washington sends word that he wishes to buy our land, he asks much of us. The Great Chief sends word that he will reserve us a place so that we can live comfortably to ourselves. He will be our father, and we will be his children. So we will consider your offer to buy our land. But it will not be easy. For this land is sacred to us.*
>
> *What is man without the beasts? If all the beasts were gone, man would die from a great loneliness of spirit. For whatever happens to the beasts soon happens to man. All things are connected.*

This we know: The earth does not belong to man; man belongs to the earth. This we know: All things are connected, like the blood which unites one family. All things are connected.

Whatever befalls the earth befalls the sons of the earth. Man did not weave a web of life; he is merely a strand in it. Whatever he does to the web, he does to himself.

But in your perishing, you will shine brightly, fired by the strength of the God who brought you to this land and, for some special purpose, gave you dominion over this land and over the red man. That destiny is a mystery to us, for we do not understand when the wild buffalo are all slaughtered, the wild horses are tamed, the secret corners of the forest heavy with the scent of many men and the view of the ripe hills blotted by talking wires. Where is the thicket? Gone. Where is the eagle? Gone. The end of living and the beginning of survival."

However, the subjective and comparative problem of interaction in civilizational elements leads the debate into a realm of philosophy. This cross-cultural flow between civilisations has led to the current debate on the nature of the environment itself. This distinction requires elaboration:

> "*The implicit, pre-conceptual categories differ from culture to culture, largely depending on time and place, which form the basis of experience. But the fact that the categories differ is also due to the ordering principle itself. The different classifications people have in different cultures are all meant to (re)present reality. They order on the basis of what they see, live and experience. Yet this experience can never be complete. Because of the very ordering principle itself, part of the outside world will always remain out of sight. Ordering is always also selective....*"[6]

The above extract focuses on the emerging standpoints of worldviews in the League of Admitted Diversity. The Indian or Hindu Model is looked at as the 'Second Order' where:

> "*.... categories manifest themselves in at least three ways in a culture. Firstly, they get densely ramified in language, such as discourses, philosophical writings, oral traditions, moral sagas or fairytales. Secondly, the institutional structures of a society are largely influenced by these categorisations. Examples are the way buildings are built or the standards by which certain jobs are perceived as highly desirable and others not. Thirdly, the deduced categories become manifest in daily habits or special cultural events. Gender roles, eating patterns, rituals, ceremonies and music festivals are all part of this.*" [7]

This ecological model is purely endogenous, and the environment is viewed as a part of a whole, i.e., the universal consciousness.

It is essential to underscore the above analysis as the basis for a consciousness-based approach to ecological studies. While the practical exercise of locating ancient roots in modern shoots would reveal the endogenous societies of the globe, the philosophical attempt to unearth the difference between the perception of 'nature' in Western and Indian religious streams assumes importance.

Western and Eastern Approaches to the Environmental Question: Echoes in Philosophy

The underlying core of the Western worldview of the Environment belongs to The New Testament in its Genesis (1:26-28), which reads thus:

> *"Then God said, "Let us make mankind in our image, in our likeness, so that they may rule over the fish in the sea and the birds in the sky, over the livestock and all the wild animals, and over all the creatures that move along the ground."*
>
> *So, God created mankind in his own image, in the image of God, he created them; male and female, he created them.*
>
> *God blessed them and said to them, "Be fruitful and increase in number; fill the earth and subdue it.*
>
> *Rule over the fish in the sea and the birds in the sky and over every living creature that moves on the ground."*

Another Biblical reference to this subject is necessary, with Psalm (8:3-7):

> *"When I consider your heavens,*
> *The work of your fingers,*
> *The moon and the stars,*
> *Which you have set in place,*
> *What is man that you are mindful of him,*
> *The son of man that you care for him?*
> *You made him a little lower than the heavenly beings*
> *And crowned him with glory and honour.*
> *You made him ruler over the works of your hands;*
> *You put everything under his feet:*

All flocks and herds, and the beasts of the field;
The birds of the air,
And the fish of the sea,
All that swims the paths of the seas."

In this remarkable voyage in destiny's path, the development and evolution of ideological tenets in terms of conquest, acquisition and resource utilisation were expounded for global consumption and adaptation. The acquisitive intellect ordained therein was indicated as follows:

> *"This monetary influence is also reflected in another characteristic of modernity, its secular nature. Monetary logic is not sympathetic to religion... Quantification, measurement reducing qualitative differences to abstract generalisations and mathematical calculations have no room for mystery. In fact, part of the intellectual excitement of the Enlightenment was precisely the demystification of the universe. Already as early as the 16th Century, Luther claimed that God's divine nature was limited to God himself and did not permeate society or politics (Armstrong, 2005: 83). Hobbes posed that after creation, God withdrew from the world. Newton, as we just saw, reduced God's thoughts to mathematical formulas. Nietzsche declared that God was dead (Armstrong, 2005: 411). And Sartre finally explained that modern man has a hole in his consciousness in the shape of God, indicating that modernity had not come without a price."*[8]

Alfred North Whitehead (1861-1947), regarded as one of the greatest Philosophers produced by the West, upon a detailed study, commented on this question almost half a century ago as follows:

> *"The primary qualities are the essential qualities of substances whose spatio-temporal relationships constitute nature. The orderliness of these relationships constitutes the order of nature. The occurrences of nature are in some way apprehended by minds, which are associated with living bodies...... which, properly speaking, are qualities of the mind alone. These sensations are projected by the mind so as to clothe appropriate bodies in external nature. Thus, the bodies are perceived as with qualities which, in reality, do not belong to them, qualities which, in fact, are purely the offspring of the mind. Thus, nature gets credit, which should, in truth, be reserved for ourselves; the rose for its scent, the nightingale for its song, and the sun for its radiance. The poets are entirely mistaken. They should address the lyrics themselves and should turn them into odes of self-congratulation on the excellency of the human mind. Nature is a dull affair, soundless, scentless, colourless; merely the hurrying of material, endless and meaningless."*[9] *(Emphasis is mine)*

This connection between the worldview and its economic model already had an *a priori* explication through Max Weber's *Protestant Ethic and the Spirit of Capitalism (1905):*

> "*...Man is dominated by the making of money, by acquisition as the ultimate purpose of his life. Economic acquisition is no longer subordinated to man as the means for the satisfaction of his material needs. This reversal of what we should call the natural relationship, so irrational from a naive point of view, is evidently as definitely a leading principle of capitalism as it is foreign to all peoples, not under capitalistic influence. At the same time, it expresses a type of feeling which is closely connected with certain religious ideas.... The earning of money within the modern economic order is, so long as it is done legally, the result and the expression of virtue and proficiency in a calling, and this virtue and proficiency are, as it is now not difficult to see, the real Alpha and Omega of Franklin's ethic, as expressed in the passages we have quoted, as well as in all his works without exception.*"[10] (Emphasis Added)

This expression of the acquisitive intellect as the core of capitalism and the growth of the modern liberal order, strengthened by globalisation and monocultures of manufacturing, have resulted in the distortion of diversity and the promotion of uniformity. The solution leads to the reverence for all creation and the necessity for a 'polylogue' rather than a dialogue simpliciter.

Towards Inclusive Ecology: Beyond the Anthropocene

The inclusive nature of Dharma and its cohesive beliefs have engaged in transdisciplinary scholarship, and the real plane of analysis in the era of Climate Change belongs to this articulation:

> "*14. ... Anthropocentrism is always human interest focussed, and non-human has only instrumental value to humans. In other words, humans take precedence and human responsibilities to non-human based benefits to humans. Ecocentrism is nature-centred where humans are part of nature and non-human has intrinsic value. In other words, human interest does not take automatic precedence and humans have obligations to non-humans independently of human interest. Ecocentrism is therefore life-centred, nature-centred where nature includes both human and non-humans.*"[11]

The imminent need for global engagement with India will be due to its philosophical contribution and resource-based support. This universal ethic of the supreme consciousness manifested through its all-embracing religion and spiritual strength, will help the globe escape from the era of 'subjugation of nature' to 'reintegration with nature', thereby heralding India's soft leadership at the helm of cultural cooperation and conflict avoidance.

NOTES

1. Ervin Laszlo, 'A Holisitic Worldview for a planetary Civilisation' in Moving Worldviews: Reshaping Sciences, Policies and Practices for endogenous sustainable development, Bertus Haverkort and Coen Reijntjes Eds., Compas Series on Worldviews and Sciences 4, Leusden, Netherlands, 2006, p. 97.
2. Ibid.
3. Fritjof Kapra, *The Web of Life: A New Synthesis of Mind and Matter*, Harper Collins, London, 1997.
4. S. Radhakrishnan, *Religion and Society*, London, Allen & Unwin, 1948, p. 106.
5. Alexander Kadakin, http://timesofindia.indiatimes.com/edit-page/LEADER-ARTICLEBRPassage-to-India-The-Coexistence-of-Multiple-Realities/articleshow/728717.cms
6. Nicole Note, "Reflections about Worldviews, the Western Worldview and intercultural polylogue" in Moving Worldviews: Reshaping Sciences, Policies and Practices for endogenous sustainable development, Bertus Haverkort and Coen Reijntjes Eds., Compas Series on Worldviews and Sciences 4, Leusden, Netherlands, 2006, p. 84.
7. Ibid., p. 85.
8. Henk Molenaar, "Communicating Worldviews: Articulating Global and Local Knowledge" in Moving Worldviews: Reshaping Sciences, Policies and Practices for endogenous sustainable development, Bertus Haverkort and Coen Reijntjes Eds., Compas Series on Worldviews and Sciences 4, Leusden, Netherlands, 2006, pp. 123-124.
9. Whitehead, *Science and the Modern World* (1925), p. 56.
10. http://xroads.virginia.edu/~HYPER/WEBER/WeberCH2.html
11. Judgment of the Supreme Court of India in *Godavarman Thirumulpad v. Union of India* (2013).

6

ANIRBAN GANGULY

Referring to a "remarkable characteristic of early Asian history," of the ancient world, and especially of Asia, until a certain era, argues pre-eminent historian of civilisation and of culture, D.P. Singhal (1925-1986), "was the receptivity to cultural ideas regardless of their nationality and lack of religious bigotry." It was uncommon to see "prejudice against a foreign belief," and if a trace of it was visible, "it was never strong enough to cause total rejection of a different faith."[1]

The "civilised people of those days," Singhal observes, "seem to have implicitly accepted the proposition that there were numerous approaches to truth and, without any false sense of pride, or violated nationalism, they readily accepted knowledge, alien or otherwise, if they thought it worthwhile."[2] This "free flow of ideas," without the constraints of a national barrier, unhampered by "preconceptions" and prejudice, "made the ancient world in some ways far more international in its cultural outlook and social behaviour than our present day society."[3]

Assessing civilisational India's contacts with countries and other civilisations on her north, east and southeast, Singhal makes an interesting comparison. He argues, for instance, that in India's relations with countries lying to her west, were primarily shaped by commerce and trade, while cultural intercourse remained a subordinated partner.[4] Ideas did cross the regions, but they did so with "goods, soldiers and travellers." Very few were undertaken "just to seek knowledge and learning." With countries lying to India's east, north and southeast, Singhal argues, "trade played a significant, but secondary role."[5]

Anirban Ganguly, Chairman, Dr. Syama Prasad Mookerjee Research Foundation & Honorary Member, Maha Bodhi Society of India.

Commerce, which initiated contact in this region, was soon "outpaced by culture" and the "marks of Indian culture" in these regions are more evident and distinct than those in the West.[6] Singhal reminds us of the perception that "India's finest contributions to human civilisation lie in Central Asia, East Asia and Southeast Asia."[7]

Both Buddhism and Hinduism played a central role in this civilisational and cultural exchange, and diffusion. Both Hinduism and Buddhism, and their proponents, demonstrated a remarkable approach. They were "never fanatical, bigoted, or obtrusive." Buddhist missionaries "never served the interests of a militant political power. In the true spirit of its faith, Buddhism prevailed peacefully through force of conviction."

One of India's greatest and most prolific of scholars of Buddhism, Rahul Sankrityayan (1893-1963), observes in a similar vein that Buddhism was "always constructive and complementary to the rightful national aims and achievements" of any civilisation. Even when civilisations were less developed, or weak, Buddhism or Buddhist missionaries never attempted to overpower, subdue, or subsume them.[8] Like Hinduism, Buddhism did not "lay claim to exclusiveness and remained exceptionally tolerant of other beliefs, and remained exceptionally tolerant of other beliefs."[9] Like Hinduism, Buddhism too "acted as a catalyst in different societies, helping them to bring out their dormant strengths and to release their creative energies." The capacities of these two religions, belief systems and philosophies, "to absorb, to impart and to fertilise, remains unique and unmatched in the history of cultural expansion,"[10] Singhal observes.

Examples abound of this synthesis across this vast region. Both, Buddhist and Hindu thought and worship were absorbed and blended in equal proportion. The worship of Ganesha, for instance, best illustrates this. It is said that the worship of Ganesha from India, travelled to distant lands along with Buddhism. In Southeast Asia, Ganesha "was worshipped as a Hindu deity, whereas in the Far East, he was adored as a Buddhist deity." From Afghanistan to Japan, Thailand to Indonesia, Cambodia to Champa, Khotan to Bali, Nepal to China, in regions where Buddhism flourished, Ganesha too has been extensively worshipped.[11]

One of India's leading linguists, philologists, polyglots and cultural philosophers, was Suniti Kumar Chatterji (1890-1977). A prolific scholar and an intellectual, Chatterji was a cultural disciple of India's Poet Laureate and civilisational thought-leader, Rabindranath Tagore. He described this spread of civilisational India's philosophies and arts, in the following way: He writes, "Indian civilisation was itself broad-based on a spirit of harmony and inclusiveness which does not regard anything human as essentially alien or repugnant, either to man or to God."[12] This fundamental approach, brought "self-respect with civilisation to the peoples inside and outside the geographical limits of India who came in touch with its vivifying influence,"[13] and at the same time also brought their own "contributions to make it richer and more universal, while they themselves participated in the deeper and wider life presented by it." The keynote of civilisational India's cultural diffusion, writes Chatterji, who was also a profound scholar of Buddhism, was inspired by "assimilation" and not "suppression" and, therefore, its achievement was "something more than that of a mere force of material civilisation or civilised organisation."[14]

Wherever it travelled, Indian philosophy and culture, Chatterji argues, "came not to destroy, but to fulfil. It came like the life-giving rain, not like the burning wind or the killing blight."[15] While certain ideology-driven belief systems have sought to establish themselves through impositions and superimpositions, Indian philosophy and culture has been intrinsically assimilative and adaptive. Evidence abounds to prove that those who "built up Indian culture and those who helped to disseminate it abroad," writes Chatterji, were moved by 'a well-understood spiritual urge to the lands beyond, to carry the message of the good of life and of the realisation of the highest good that they had found through a deliberate quest on the soil of India."[16]

Chatterji movingly describes this unique method of evolving shared values and their shared cultural, ethical and philosophical expressions. The sense of the sacredness of all life, the profound philosophical ideas, answers to some of the fundamental questions that have exercised mankind over the ages, were transmitted through a multitude of ways through the "wisdom, the intellectual quest and the self-discipline of the Brahmana mingled with the all-embracing compassion and the active charity of the Buddhist *Sramana*" and came across as "refreshing streams for the parched soul of man over a greater part of Asia." It was this "sense of kinship with humanity as a whole (*Vasudhaiva Kutumbakam*) and the yearning for the happiness and salvation of all men formed a great impetus and inspiration to send forth the Buddhist and the Brahmana teachers with the message of the *Rsis* and the Jinas into distant and inaccessible lands."[17]

A compelling urge to share certain truths and realisations inspired this civilisational mobility. The truths that she had obtained for herself, the means of realising those truths, allowed civilisational India to aspire to share and to disseminate. It was thus, in the words of Chatterji, in a "spirit of joyful participation," that civilisational India's messengers peregrinated "into countries known and unknown and gave of her treasure to the nations."[18]

Indian thought and culture, argues Chatterji, spread not in the wake of a "world-conquering king who carried at the head of his legions fire and sword, barbarities and sufferings innumerable. India never made herself manifest to the outside world in the person of a world-shaker.... Her "*digvijaya*" or "world-conquest" was the conquest of Truth and Law – the "*dharma – vijaya*" which was the ideal of Asoka, the greatest and truest Indian king of history..." Civilisational India emerged in the old world, as a "*Kalyana-Mitra*", a friend and fellow in the collective quest for the highest good.

Suniti Kumar Chatterji, spoke with authority and from experience. He was an extensive world traveller, immersing himself in civilisational studies as a National Professor of India, writing and speaking extensively. More importantly for our discussion, he accompanied Rabindranath Tagore on a historic four-month-long journey across Southeast Asia, closely observing, mingling with and recording local customs, practices and systems.

One of the best and most enduring examples of an Indian teacher, who travelled outward to spread India's civilisational knowledge, which was much sought after, was that of Acharya Atisa Dipankara Srijnana. The king of Tibet, Ye-she-Od, sent his emissaries to plead with Atisa, then teaching in the Grand Vihara of Vikramshila, which had become a "great and successful rival of Nalanda", and where, "thousands of students not only from different parts of India, but also from outside countries", came to study. They wished to persuade Atisa to come to Tibet, "it would reform the Buddhist church..."[19]

After a long and relentless persuasion, Atisa decided to proceed to Tibet. When he reached Tibet, the king's welcome of Atisa was unprecedented. Such was the honour in which Indian teachers were looked upon. We have a description from Rahul Sankrityayan that is worth reproducing.

When Dipankara entered Tibet; one hundred picked soldiers on white horses headed by their general welcomed him. In welcoming him the king's representative expressed their feeling thus: "O greatest Indian Teacher, your coming to our country is not less than the coming of a God. We shall ever remain thankful to you for this act of compassion. No doubt Tibet is not as fortunate as India as far as the spread of Dharma is concerned, but the Tibetans have their own special characteristic. During summer it is not as hot as in India; and during winter its narrow hill villages are sufficiently warm.... We Tibetans are always ready to serve you."[20]

Atisa lived in Tibet for fourteen years, travelling and spreading knowledge, infusing fresh perspectives into Buddhism. He wrote "more than forty-three works on Mahayana Buddhism and other subjects, and more than one hundred and twenty-seven on tantric themes. Besides these he translated many Sanskrit works into Tibetan and revised an equal number of such as was translated before him."[21] While in Tibet, Atisa wrote one of his most enduring works, his magnum opus, "*Bodhipathapradipa*".[22]

Atisa Dipankara is a key figure in the religious history of both India and Tibet. "He was about the last of the great Buddhist *acaryas* in India and though not the first, he is remembered in Tibetan tradition itself as by far the greatest of teacher-reformers. From this follows also his stature in Buddhist world-history.[23] His life and legacy remain a concrete example of how Indian teachers, carrying the torch of knowledge, lit fires of reformation and rejuvenation in distant lands, preserving societies and civilisations through shared beliefs and values. Atisa's is a well-known and recorded contribution. There are numerous like him among Buddhist and Hindu teachers who followed a similar line of action from India in her civilisational past. To this day, Atisa is revered and followed across Tibet, China and Mongolia, besides other Buddhist-dominant countries as a whole.

In Mongolia, in modern times, Venerable Kushak Bakula Rinpoche (1918-2003), a monk-diplomat and leader, much like Atisa Dipankara, played a crucial and historic role in the revival and preservation of Buddhism in Mongolia, re-opening ancient monasteries, arranging for the sacred Buddha Relics to be taken to that country from India and in guiding a peaceful transition to democracy. Perhaps the only monk-diplomat, Bakula Rinpoche, carried on a tradition that was inherent to civilisational India in the past. It demonstrated how India had evolved a framework of exchange and assimilation through teachers who knew the imperative of shared values.[24]

In civilisational India's contact with the world, one sees Arnold Toynbee's three responses, narrowed down to two. There was no "recoil" where civilisational India's knowledge, culture and philosophies touched. The dominant responses were "adaptation" and "synthesis". This synthesis evolved into an entire scheme and framework of shared values and beliefs. Wherever Indians went and settled in this era, they infused their culture and civilisation. "In turn, they were influenced by the indigenous culture, laying thus the foundation of a new culture in the region."[25]

On the eve of his visit to Southeast Asia, Tagore spoke of how the "real wealth of India was never kept hidden, like an old deed in an iron safe," and that the "only true expression of India was in all that she gave openly and freely. The surplus of her cultural life, which she scattered everywhere, was the core of her personality. Through our capacity to give our real assets to others we earn the title to call the 'outsider' our own."[26] Tagore's letters from Java, "*Java Jatrir Patra*", written in 1927, abound with descriptions of this assimilation and synthesis. Communicating from Karang Asem, he writes of his wonder at realising every moment "how largely the life of these people is intertwined with Hindu beliefs and rituals. And yet Hinduism in its pure form", was "nowhere to be seen; mingled with the nature of this people, it has taken a peculiar shape of which the gestures are Hindu, the body Malayan…in spite of the differences in detail from things India, there was, nevertheless, a similarity of attitude."

Tagore founded his university, "Visva-Bharati", in Santiniketan, in Bengal, as a modern version of Nalanda of Vikramshila, a centre of knowledge and learning, which would invite learners from across civilisations. He had hoped that this centre of learning would also evolve as a meeting point of cultures and civilisations. Addressing the Indian community at the Phya Thai Palace Grounds in Bangkok, Tagore reminded that segregation was 'the worst thing that can happen to any country. A "nation that is too occupied with her own internal affairs, and does not contribute her surplus of culture to the outside world, is doomed and will fail in getting even that for which it hankers."[27]

Addressing a distinguished gathering at the historic Dusit Palace, in the presence of the King and Queen of Siam, in 1927, Tagore spoke of a "common mentality" of Asia. He referred to "one type of continental culture, which was the result of co-operation among various peoples in the past." Asia "must realise this great continental culture of hers", Tagore exhorted his audience, "if she was to regain her self-consciousness."[28] This creation of a continental culture, evolved through centuries of cooperation, exchange and assimilation, was a shared consciousness. This continental culture will eventually define and shape the Asian century as articulated by Prime Minister Narendra Modi.

Another iconic and revered personality in Mongolia and across the world for his Buddhist scholarship, was Dr Raghu Vira (1902-1963). Hemust be remembered on this occasion. Mongolians and Mongolian intelligentsia continue to speak and mention his name with reverence. Dr Raghu Vira was a profound scholar, a public intellectual, a polymath, an outstanding, unparalleled scholar of Buddhism and an active political leader. He was among the first to establish a civilisational connect between Mongolia and India. To a question that some ask, as to why Samvad-III is being held in Mongolia, Raghu Vira's words best describe the India-Mongolia civilisational connect of an Asian century based on shared values. He created a lasting corpus of these values. As president of the India-Mongolia Friendship Society, he renewed civilisational linkages between the two nations. He was the author of the first Mongolian-Sanskrit and Sanskrit-Mongolian Dictionary, compiled after a long and painstaking study of Classical Mongolian translations and original Sanskrit texts.

It would be worthwhile to look at some of Raghu Vira's descriptions in our quest to draw an actionable narrative leading towards the creation of an Asian Century of shared values and Dharma. He refers to India as the "perpetual giver of gifts", that did not exploit, did not dominate and did not inflict defeats. Indian missionaries, argues Raghu Vira:

> "...Without the European sword or a book of dogmas in their hands, sallied forth over mountainous crags, over tortuous streams, through deserts and snowy peaks, over long distances, occupying not days and but months and years and reached far-off ends of the world, landed among foreign peoples, learnt their languages and becoming one of them, they spread their own fragrance, their own radiance and captivated their hearts and inspired their lives, moulded their conduct, gave them arts and ideas of arts...Work and unselfishness, raising themselves and then raising others, have characterised the work of the Indian missions extending over centuries and millenniums."[29]

Dr Raghu Vira lyrically describes the expressions of a shared cultural heritage. He was surprised to "an extraordinary degree" when he travelled tothe interior of Mongolia and found herdsman "interested in the literal theories of Dandin's 'Kavyadarsha', or wanting clarification of some points in Panini's phonetics...."[30]

Dr Raghu Vira continues with drawing links and points of connection, of shared values and of expression. "One of the mountains in Mongolia is named Sumeru, another Vaidurya, a lake is named after Durga. Yamantaka, Mahakala, Yama, Kali, are worshipped among all Mongols, the Goddess Tara is worshipped and cherished by men and women, and children…The national banner of Outer Mongolia is known under the ancient title Svayambhu, pronounced Soyombo…. Stories of King Bhoja and Vikramaditya are prevalent under the name of Arji Bhurji, that is the form that has endeared itself to the tongues of the Mongols. Pronounced in our way it will be Raja Bhoja. The small lyrics of Kalidasa, Meghaduta has also found a place of honour in Mongolian literature; similarly, stories of *Pancatantra*."[31]

He found among Mongolians, "much hospitality and great affection for India among the Mongolian people…" We still feel that very strongly. "Our way of reciprocating their love can find expression in many ways, one of them being the study of their language and literature…" Raghuvira makes a wonderful case here of shared and assimilated values. He says, "Their place in history is already assured… they have been builders of great empires from the Pacific to the plains of Hungary, they're have been great authors, thinkers, artists and sculptors among them…."[32] A foundation of mutuality and sacredness is what inspires the edifice of shared values. The Asian Century must be based on such a foundation.

That civilisational propensity, normal in the past, of sharing and of exchange, of renewing and relaying the linkages must be renewed among Buddhist and Hindu scholars, and thought-leaders. In Mongolia, one cannot but refer to such a proposition made by Dr Raghu Vira, just as India was becoming independent. "The ancient showed us". Dr Raghu Vira reminded us:

> "…the two-fold way of maintaining the unity of culture, the wandering teachers and the yearning pilgrims, one anxious to teach, the other anxious to grasp and learn. The system must be resuscitated with vigour…Political boundaries have been changing for the last 2000 years, ever since Indian culture spread to these countries. Different dynasties have ruled over them, sometimes they have been free and sometimes dependent. But Indian culture has come down as one continuous flow. The only tragic thing has been that for centuries past people have altogether lost consciousness of their connection with India…The last pilgrims from China came to India in the tenth century. After that Islamic hordes became a permanent barrier for nay civilised and peaceful intercourse between Central Asia and India. India has also stopped sending her missions to these northern lands…The glory of India lies in the distribution of spiritual gifts…"[33]

Dr Raghu Vira calls for renewing the pilgrim and teachers trail and linkages. Indians themselves, he suggests, "must accept the role of pilgrims to these lands where vast and grand monuments of her ancient culture stand, proclaiming their eternal message to the world... We should be starting shiploads of pilgrims and teachers to all these countries year after year carrying with them good-will and understanding..."[34]

In the early years after independence, Dr Syama Prasad Mookerjee (1901-1953), one of India's leading statesman, educationists, Member of Parliament, a public leader and President of the Maha Bodhi Society of India, spoke of India assuming the "role of the spiritual mother" for these countries. He called for re-establishing "bonds of friendship and understanding with them with a true sense of humility and responsibility."[35]

Speaking of a dominant characteristic of the civilisation that India had evolved, Dr Raghu Vira observes that it was a civilisation that 'gave the greatest amount of freedom of thought and action. The human conscience was so moulded, that there was room in it for appreciating a variety of views, ideas and actions. "A general theory of action and thought was formulated so that there could be nothing which would shock and repulse categorically a new and un-known thing."[36] This led civilisational India eventually being recognised as a "Kalyan-Mitra" in the ancient world. In the present, that must also inspire the movement forward to evolve a framework of action based on shared values cultural and spiritual heritage.

This long, but by no means exhaustive list of profound Indian thought-leaders, who described India's civilisational linkages, also spoke of shared values, and called for a renewal of that approach. It gives an insight into their thinking and their identities as peripatetic internationalists who were firmly rooted in their cultural and civilisational essence. Their thoughts, proposed frameworks and vision remain contemporary and can serve to delineate a future roadmap towards realising the Asian Century of shared values and creative action for greater global welfare.

In Mongolia, the third edition of Samvad struck a deep chord. Leaders, both political and religious, saw it as a great confluence from which will emerge a refreshed civilisational partnership. Despite the many vicissitudes and challenges, the Mongolians saw Samvad as a taking forward to the next step that which Prime Minister Narendra Modi initiated in 2015. The Speaker of the Mongolian Parliament, the Prime Minister of Mongolia, leading Buddhist monks led by the Venerable Khamba Lama, head of the Gandan Monastery (a centre of Mongolian Buddhism), who was the co-host, were all active participants in this congregation.

Why Mongolia, some have asked? The region, which was once central to civilisational India had, over the centuries, receded in memory and is now once more gravitating back towards centrality. In 2015, Prime Minister Modi undertook a historic visit to the country and imparted a modern shape to our ancient connect. Iconic Kushak Bakula Rinpoche's centenary year in 2018 and its fitting observance brought this region, its cultural and strategic importance to the centre-stage once more. Samvad-III is being held within a year of the observance of Bakula Rinpoche's centenary.

Samvad has an ideational dimension. It also aims to reach out to a geographical and geo-cultural space. A space which, in the civilisational past, was an active entrepot of ideas and of aspirations, a carrefour where shared-values emerged and which encouraged an assimilative synthesis.

In course of his address, the Japanese Ambassador to Mongolia, spoke about the Indo-Pacific being a powerhouse. For us now, as for civilisational India in the past, the Indo-Pacific is our natural civilisational sphere; and through Samvad, the Indo-Pacific is seen and recognised as a Dharmic Civilisational Zone. The foundations of the emergence of the Asian Century can be envisaged and nurtured in this zone.

In India today, a multidimensional and multifaceted transformation is taking place. It is a transformation taking place through value-based governance. Prime Minister Modi speaks of the "Asian Century". He says, "The 21st century is to be the Asian Century" and one of the civilisational roles of Samvad can be to define and articulate that Asian Century. The fulcrum of the Asian Century is going to be the Indo-Pacific, and in that, the traditions, the religions, the faiths and the values that converge through Samvad, are going to be the defining factors.

Governance in India today exudes and radiates compassion – "Karuna." It is compassion that defines governance in India today. Prime Minister Modi speaks about "*Jan Bhagidari*", that is, "people's participation", and "*Jan Andolan*", "people's movement". Any fundamental transformation that is taking place in Indian society today is being done through "people's participation" and "people's movement". That is the essence of fabric of Indic-Eastern Democracy. Two hundred and fifty million people have been lifted out of multidimensional poverty in India over the last one decade.[37] Millions are gaining access, for the first time, to clean water and sanitation, lives are being saved and empowered.

Empowerment and inclusion, nationalism and development, are going hand-in-hand. A vast number of lives are being altered in India today. There is an emphasis on equity and there is an insistence on ending discrimination. The emphasis on development and the quest for rediscovering our cultural and civilisational roots, are going hand-in-hand. There is no conflict between these two approaches. It is evolving, in a sense, a framework of governance for the future.

We have often spoken about human rights, which is very important, but obviously, we also realise that there are narratives of human rights. There is a narrative of human rights that has been shaped in and emanates from the West, but we must also recognise that no narrative, in this age of universal democracy, can be imposed on the others. We need to evolve the concept and framework of Asian human rights, of an Asian dimension to human rights. We speak about rights, and it is legitimate, but in a democracy, there has to be a sense of duty. "*Lok Adhikar*", human rights, is perfect, it is legitimate, but there has to be a sense of "*Lok Kartavya*", citizenship duty.

A number of conflicts start, number of conflicts that are pushed through, are because of this exclusive emphasis on rights, with no commensurate emphasis on duties. The Dharmic civilisational thought of governance with its roots in civilisational India, gives equal weightage to this concept of duty – *Lok Kartavya*. Hindu and Buddhist masters and teachers have also emphasised this dimension. The evolution of shared values must be based on that sense of collective duty – a duty for positive action for our present and for the future. The schema of the Asian Century must be driven by that deeper sense of duty.

The major challenge today before the leadership in Asia and of the world, the major challenge to the evolution of shared civilisational values is the scourge of terrorism. Terrorism is the greatest obstacle to Samvad – dialogue and exchange, and there can be no good terrorism, or bad terrorism. Terrorism is the most anti-human and destructive genie that has been let out of the bottle today.[38]

We should all come together, and Samvad must take a clear position on terrorism. Samvad must also have a very clear articulation on freedom of movement, on freedom of thought, exchange of thought, on freedom of navigation, physical as well as ideational, all across this region of the Indo-Pacific. There can be no hegemony; there can be no monopoly, there can be no control, and there can be no ideology, which emerges here, or takes root which is anti-human. This will facilitate the shaping of the Asian Century of Dharma-Dhamma.

A convention or a declaration on terrorism is essential. We have to realise that values can only be shared when they can be preserved. Values can only be impactful when they are perpetuated and nurtured. In order to do that, we need to come out extremely strongly against those elements, which promote terrorism and violence, those elements who support those who promote terrorism and violence, and those elements who would like to perpetuate a hegemonic f way of life, thought and action.

If the 21st century is to be truly the Asian Century, it can only be shaped by the ideals of the Upanishads and by the essence of the message of Lord Buddha. One of the most renowned monks of modern India, Swami Ranganathananda, of the Ramakrishna Order, observes that "Buddha stands closest to the spirit of the Upanishads. In fact, it is not possible to appreciate the life and teachings of Buddha adequately without understanding the spirit of the Upanishads."[39]

It is the path of the future, it is the path of sustainability, and it is the path of lasting solutions to complex and festering global problems and challenges. The Asian Century has to be Dharma and Dhamma inspired and driven. An illustrious array of civilisational thought-leaders in India and across Asia have often aspired to this new era. Legions of teachers and seekers have criss-crossed the ancient world on ancient routes, without prejudice and inhibition, driven by the urge for new light and thought. They aspired to disseminate these without condition, or restraint across continents and civilisations, with the hope that the era of shared values and of shared action would be a perpetual one. The rekindling of that urge and of that ancient spirit would not only be a true tribute to these forgotten and remembered seekers and teachers, but would also lay a firm and dynamic foundation to the edifice of the Asian Century.

Therein lies the deeper essence and the *raison d'être* of Samvad.

NOTES

1 D.P. Singhal, *Buddhism in East Asia*, New Delhi: Books & Books Publishers, 1984.
2 Ibid.
3 Ibid.
4 Ibid.
5 Ibid.
6 Ibid.
7 Ibid.
8 Rahul Sankrityayan, 'Renaissance of Buddhism in the East,' in *Selected Essays*, New Delhi: People's Publishing House, 1984.
9 Singhal, op.cit.
10 Ibid.
11 See e.g. M.K.Dhavalikar, 'Ganesa Beyond the Indian Frontiers' in *India's Contribution to World Thought & Culture*, (Editor-in-Charge, Lokesh Chandra) Chennai: Vivekananda Kendra Prakashan, 1970 (reprint 2003).
12 Suniti Kumar Chatterji, *Select Papers – Angla-Nibandha-Chayana*, Vol.2, New Delhi: People's Publishing House, 1979.
13 Ibid.
14 Ibid.
15 Ibid.
16 Ibid.
17 Ibid.
18 Ibid.
19 Rahul Sankrityayan, 'Life of Acharya Dipankara Srijnana', in *Selected Essays*, op.cit.
20 Ibid.
21 Ibid.
22 Ibid.
23 Alaka Chattopadhyay, *Atisa and Tibet: Life and Works of Dipamkara Srijana in relation to the History and Religion of Tibet*, Kolkata: Indian Studies: Past & Present, 1967.
24 Ganesh Malhotra, 'Architect of Modern Ladakh', in *Daily Excelsior*, January 14, 2018, also see, D.C.Ahir, *The Pioneers of Buddhist Revival in India*, New Delhi: Satguru Publications, 1989.
25 D.P. Singhal, *India and World Civilisation*, (reprint 1993), New Delhi: Rupa Publications, 2014.
26 Rabindranath Tagore, *Letters from Java*, (Rabindranath Tagore's Tour of Southeast Asia, 1927), (Edited and Translated by Supriya Roy), Kolkata: Visva Bharati Publishing Dept, 2010.
27 Ibid.
28 Rabindranath Tagore's address as reported in the Siam Observer, Friday, October 14, 1927, in Shakti Das Gupta, *Tagore's Asian Outlook*, (Edited Shekhar Dasgupta), Gurgaon: Zorba Books, 2nd edition, 2021.
29 Raghu Vira, *India and Asia – a Cultural Symphony* (collection of some notes, articles, poems and letters), New Delhi: International Academy of Indian Culture, 1978.
30 Ibid.

31 Ibid.
32 Ibid.
33 Ibid.
34 Ibid.
35 Anirban Ganguly, '*Pali: The Civilisational Bridge Connecting India to Its Global Buddhist Heritage*', 15 November, 2024, News18 accessed at: https://www.news18.com/opinion/opinion-pali-the-civilisational-bridge-connecting-india-to-its-global-buddhist-heritage-9121415.html
36 Raghu Vira, *India and Asia – a Cultural Symphony,* op. cit.
37 '25 crore people in India came out of multidimensional poverty in 9 years: Report', *India Today*, January 16, 2024.
38 Prime Minister Narendra Modi in course of his various address at the UNGA and other multilateral global forums has flagged this fallacious distinction.
39 Swami Ranganathananda, *Bhagavan Buddha and Our Heritage*, Kolkata: Advaita Ashrama, 1991.

(This paper is a version based on the address delivered at Samvad-III at Ulaan Bataar, Mongolia, in September 2019)

7

DAIKO MATSUYAMA

Thank you for inviting me to join spiritual leaders from across Asia at this wonderful conference. As a Buddhist priest in Japan, I would like to talk about the role that Buddhism can play in the world, and about what we are doing to fulfil that responsibility.

Nowadays, we often seem to be living in two separate worlds. People are divided by dualism: yes or no, good or bad, friend or enemy. This can happen around the world and maybe even in your own house.

This is a scary way to exist. No matter who wins for the moment, the war is never over. This problem is not only modern but also ancient. Two thousand five hundred years ago, the Buddha confronted the same dilemma. He taught about escaping from the trap of dualism. Dividing things up is easy, but – as you know – the world itself is not so simple. Consider the most basic thing: yourself. Are you good or bad ... or rather a combination of good and bad? If I ask you tomorrow, would your answer still be the same? Things change over time. Nothing is permanent. All things must pass. The Buddha taught us to see holistically, to unify rather than divide. That is the way to eliminate conflict.

Our modern age is full of contradictions. Values are spread both horizontally and vertically. We can see examples of horizontal diversity in the inclusion of sexual and racial minorities. In many societies, stereotypes are fading. People are less likely to be pushed to the side. Of course, that is not true everywhere, but I think we can say that it is the general direction.

What's important is seeing things as one, not two; united, not divided. If something seems divided, draw a bigger circle around it in order to make it united.

Daiko Matsuyama, Deputy Head Priest, Taizo-in Zen Buddhist Temple, Japan

The verticalisation of values is also progressing at lightning speed. For example: Universal Studios Japan is rated 4.0. Tokyo Disneyland is 4.4. Taizoin, my temple, is 4.5. Do you know what I'm talking about? These are the ratings on an internet rating site. As I'm telling you this, I can hear the voices of my two daughters saying, "No way! USJ and Disneyland are much more interesting than Taizoin!" It's hard for me to disagree, but I prefer not to think of things in that way. I don't believe amusement parks and temples can be evaluated on the same scale.

The same is true for food. You may be able to compare different ramen shops. But internet restaurant sites compare ramen, French, Chinese, and all sorts of cuisines side by side. How about universities: which is better, Harvard or MIT? Some organisations rank the universities of the world, comparing those in Kyoto to those in Bangalore to those in Ulaanbaatar. But are they really the same thing, or – like theme parks and temples – different kinds of institutions, with their own distinct qualities? This presents us with another contradiction of sorts: values are spreading horizontally but also being stacked vertically.

Many people wonder about the right way to live in this contradictory world, and what to rely on. The Buddha taught that the world doesn't determine meaning for us. We determine the meaning of the world. If something is fun, it's not fun because someone else says it is. It's fun because you find it fun. The food at a restaurant is not delicious because it's gotten good reviews online. It's delicious because you find it delicious.

Rather than being influenced by other people's evaluations and behaviour, cherish your own instincts. That is true "freedom." Other people's evaluations are valid for them. Yours are valid for you. Don't look outside. Look inside. Shakespeare said, "To thine own self be true." So did the Buddha.

Of course, the Buddha didn't know about internet rating sites when he spoke 2500 years ago. But he did know about human nature ... the nature of people then and now. Buddhist teachings and Asian philosophy can greatly contribute to this modern world, filled with apparent contradictions.

A major challenge that we all face is protecting our environment. The world's population continues to grow, and the earth is struggling to support a huge number of people. It is an issue that both unites us and divides us. We all share this planet, but we do so with different economic resources. Disparities have led to social problems and unrest. Various movements around the world are promoting ways to meet these challenges.

One of the most promising approaches involves Sustainable Development Goals, called SDGs for short. The movement went mainstream when it was embraced by the United Nations. In essence, it calls for sharing resources and reconsidering individual consumption, especially in economically developed countries. Practices such as car sharing, bicycle sharing, and reusing goods over the Internet are growing year by year. Returning to simpler times may be impossible. People are accustomed to convenience, but convenience doesn't demand unlimited consumption. As SDGs spread, production may slow down. On the other hand, resources will be used effectively. I think this will contribute to a sustainable society.

Various related initiatives have begun in Buddhist temples in Japan. One example is the "temple snack club" – Otera Oyatsu Kurabu in Japanese. It is staffed by young monks. Temples receive daily offerings of food from believers and followers. We are grateful for all these, but – especially at large temples – we often get more than we can use. Throwing them away would be a terrible waste. Until recently though, we haven't had an easy way to redistribute them.

That's where the Otera Oyatsu Kurabu comes in. It brings these offerings to economically disadvantaged families and single-parent families ... especially to children who don't get enough to eat daily. This not only makes use of valuable resources, but it also embraces people who are impoverished and, sometimes, alienated from society. The program is Buddhist mercy and charity put into action.

We also can act across borders. I am currently involved in a project initiated by the Royal Queen Mother of Bhutan. It is aimed at supporting temple restoration in that country. Bhutan has a shortage of specialists in this sort of work. Somehow, construction and maintenance techniques did not get passed on over the years there. So, the country often relies on workers from neighbouring India and Bangladesh. The lack of homegrown specialists, however, has made it hard to keep temples in good repair. Sometimes, these places of faith had to be destroyed and rebuilt.

In this case, the solution for the future may be found in the past. Japanese carpenters have temple repair traditions that have been maintained across generations. Their methods are more efficient than the alternative of scrap-and-build. Her Majesty invited Japanese craftsmen to come repair existing temple structures so that they could continue to be used for hundreds of years. She also hoped Bhutanese people, especially Buddhist monks would learn these techniques and that, eventually, they could take care of necessary repairs themselves.

Japanese carpenters like to say, "If your building isn't older than the age of the tree, you can't say that you had a first-class carpenter." Most Japanese temples are made of wood, but fine carpentry allows the buildings to stand much longer than the age of the wood itself. For example, the main hall of my temple, Taizo-in, was built 420 years ago. We do major repairs once every 200 years, but even those make use wood from more than four centuries ago. Maybe the building will last 500 years.

For the Bhutan project, I consulted a specialist from a company that repairs Japanese temples, shrines, and castles. We've had Japanese personnel work in Bhutan for about two years. I'm happy to say that the repairs are almost finished. A completion ceremony will be held next month, and I'm looking forward to going there to mark the occasion.

By sharing conservation technologies across borders, we've conserved resources and supported important cultural activities. Moreover, to use the modern phrase, we've also helped transfer the technology. Activities of this sort can bring people in different places together and influence the way they act and think about one another.

Conflict resolution and environmental conservation: these two goals can become one. It's an admirable idea, but if it remains as nothing more than a thought, society will not change. Society can be transformed by putting these ideas into action, through mechanisms that allow everyone to be involved. I believe that Buddhist benevolence can contribute to renewing the world – our world – making it better and better.

8

Khen Rinpoche Tashi Tsering

This short paper on conflict avoidance is based on the structure used by the historical Buddha Gautama in his very first teachings to his first five disciples. These teachings have an extremely simple yet profound and clear structure. The underlying message is that everything is underpinned by two inseparable attributes: cause and effect. In every phenomenon, every event, and everything that takes place, individually, collectively, environmentally and so forth, there are clear cause-effect relationships. Without the cause, the result cannot exist; moreover, there is a clear measure of interconnectedness. Our internal thoughts and emotions give rise to our behaviours and our actions, all of which are interconnected with what we experience physically, mentally and also environmentally. So, there is this very clear message from within these very first teachings of the Buddha that everything is interconnected, or, to use another term, interdependent.

I. Recognition or Awareness of the Existence of Conflicts (The 1st Noble Truth)

The very first thing we need to do to understand the problems we humans face is to see and understand in depth the conflicts within individuals as well as within the community, within the country as well as between countries, and so forth. For example, we need to seriously examine the present conflicts in the world, from the level of identity politics, how we relate to society, how people are forming groups to discriminate against others, how civil wars occur, and how environmental disasters arise. The first step is to make ourselves fully aware of these conflicts, both individually and collectively, bringing them to

---

Khen Rinpoche Tashi Tsering, Abbot, Sera Mey Monastic University, India.

our full awareness so that they become at the forefront of our minds, individually, socially, and collectively. Through that awareness, as humans, we can create the causes and take the initiative to solve such conflicts. For example, if we look at the environment and currently what's happening in Brazil with the burning Amazon forest, although we don't know exactly who caused the fire that led to such widespread damage, that is a very big environmental disaster, not just for this generation but for many generations to come, with thousands of hectares of forests lost that had been evolving over hundreds of years. Raising awareness of such disasters is something very important, not just to small groups of individuals but to the community at large, so that people, in general, do not treat such disasters as merely something to look at on television, only to be switched off and forgotten about. Similar to that is what is happening with immigration problems in different countries, with different races and different skin colours. Again, these are problems that are very important for us to be fully aware of and understand how they arise. And these conflicts are not just 21st-century conflicts. Problems essentially similar to these conflicts and their nature have been with us for hundreds of years, and coming to a collective awareness of these is something very important, just as the Buddha taught in his first teachings, the First Noble Truth of Suffering, when he said of dukkha, suffering, that his followers should be fully aware of the nature of dukkha. And to become fully aware of the pervasiveness of suffering is very important, not just as symptoms, not just as a surface, peripheral problem, not just as something immediate right here and now, but as something to be understood within the overall picture of the conflicts to be understood. And that is as Buddha said to his first five followers: suffering is everywhere; and we should be aware of it; it should be understood in its full nature. It is the same at our present time, individually as well as collectively, we should understand the nature of the conflicts we face and their full destructive potential.

II. Recognition and Determination to Abandon the Causes of Conflicts (The 2nd Noble Truth)

In coming to understand the nature of conflict, it is human nature to want to search for what these have developed out of where the conflicts have arisen from. Either out of the grasp of our history or our natural curiosity, and whether grounded in religious belief or not, we all know that self-centredness, selfishness, greed, and anger are always the sources of conflict. That they are such clear sources of trouble is something we can all agree on, whatever level of education we acquire. And this is the essence of Buddha's second noble truth, the Noble Truth of the Origin of Suffering, where he clearly stated that the origins of dukkha are within us, not something purely outside but within us; and, in particular, they are related to our distorted mental states. So, in understanding the nature of conflicts, we need to understand the causes that gave rise to them; then, we will be in a position to work towards avoiding those causes, reducing and, if possible, eliminating the causes of such conflicts. Again, just as the Buddha stated, the origins of dukkha should be abandoned in the case of the individual, these being those distorted mental states, such as attachment, aversion, anger, and ignorance, which the Buddha stated are the main causes of dukkha, in that first noble truth, the truth of suffering. Similarly, the conflicts we face individually and collectively have causes, and these causes should, at least at the practical level, be minimised and reduced, both individually and collectively. And here again, when we talk about collective reduction and, if possible, eliminating the causes of the conflicts, the first step has to be at the individual level, recognising first within the individuals, within ourselves, those distorted mental states, those deep-rooted anger, deep-rooted hatred, deep-rooted disagreement, deep-rooted desire for revenge. These should slowly be sorted out, and that will then slowly reach to the community level and then the society level. All talk about the community level, society or collective levels and how to change it has always to start at the individual level, and that is the second stage. That is what the Buddha taught as the second noble truth: the Noble Truth of the Origins of Suffering and that these should be abandoned.

III. Confidence and Recognition that Conflicts can be Resolved (The 3rd Noble Truth)

At the same time, it is very important and helpful, individually and collectively, to have the confidence – a certainty that conflicts can be resolved, that they can be solved, and that they can be eliminated – within the individual, within the small society and the wider society. And developing that kind of confidence, an unshakeable determination to achieve change for the better, is very important, as Buddha stated in relation to the third noble truth, the Noble Truth of Cessation: that cessation of suffering and the origins of suffering should be experienced. That means individually the cessation of all suffering and cessation of the origins of suffering can be experienced, and that is here again in Buddha's teachings. He constantly stated that every human being has the potential and the ability; we have the seeds from which the ability to overcome suffering and the origins of suffering can grow and continue growing. Here, similarly in the conflicts we face, for example, in the present time, there are lots of challenges we are facing in many parts of the world, yet these challenges, these conflicts and difficulties can be resolved, for we all have the potential for change enabling them to be resolved. So, there are seeds for change and development within us that we can nurture to bring about that change.

Because we are human beings, we have suffered individual and collective sufferings; indeed, we have had great experiences in the past. When we think about the 1st World War and the 2nd World War, and in the nearer wars in Iran and Afghanistan, so much suffering is being gone through. But we can learn from those experiences, and by learning from them, we can build a determination that having such seeds and potential for change – and from it, the ability to solve conflicts – should be put to use. The third stage, the determination that there is a way out, is something very important to foster, both individually and collectively. And that is the third noble truth: the cessation of suffering should be experienced.

IV. Searching and Applying means and Methods to Overcome Conflicts (The 4th Noble Truth)

Then, the fourth stage is the actual remedy: the means and methods to adopt in order to avoid and to resolve the conflict. And here it is again, very much at the individual level, that we have to start. We have to build the recognition of suffering and determination that the suffering is not inevitable but can be abandoned, and from that inner resolution, we will individually have more understanding of others, others' experiences, others' feelings, others' needs, others' feelings; and that will be extremely important as that carries up to the level of our communities, our societies. Without that kind of capacity, without that kind of ability to understand others' feelings, others' thoughts, and others' rights, we will continue to face difficulties. So, development is an essential step in moving towards the solution to be achieved.

And again, here in the four noble truths, there is the noble eight-fold path, and within the eight-fold path is what in modern times is called mindfulness, which is now famous and increasingly widespread. Although the very popular form of mindfulness may not be exactly what the Buddha taught as one of the noble eight-fold paths, when we are mindful – mindful of our actions, of what is going on in our thoughts, emotions, mental states, and also mindful of other beings' feelings, thoughts – we may then develop real action, not just mindfulness, but real action. And again, in the eightfold path, Buddha set out as one of the paths, "right action", where right action includes actions such as realising that all beings want to be happy; all beings prosper if treated with kindliness, compassion and respect; caring for others and putting their welfare higher than one's own is the source of long-term contentment; and then from such reflections determining that one's behaviour should put these realisations into practice. A further path within Buddha's eightfold path is the necessity of having "right intention", having intention not just for oneself to have prosperity and so on, but also having the intention to include in one's activities the securing of the wellbeing of others, and not just others right here and now in our generation but also in generations to come. That is a goal we should take on for ourselves, to educate ourselves in what we want to achieve, to be able to create the causes and conditions for others to understand. Individually building that kind of right action, having the right intention, taking that kind of initiative, that kind of action, all of these will gradually, accumulatively spread through communities and so reach to others and give rise to the most effective means and methods to ensure conflict avoidance.

So that is what I can see as the structure for how we need to work individually and collectively for conflict avoidance and conflict resolution, as well as to develop solutions to the other challenges we face. In this structure, I hope you will find that the structure of the four noble truths is illuminating both for its application to us as individuals and collectively.

9

KWAAK YOUNG-HOON

Thank you for your kind invitation to participate in the Samvad III in Ulaanbaatar. We are having a "Dialogue on Peaceful Coexistence, Inter-religious Understanding and Interdependent Sustainability." After our serious dialogue, I hope we will have the **Ulaanbaatar Ultimatum** as a timely manifestation to deal with the two most critical issues facing our world today – Human Conflicts and Environmental Degradation.

Last week, the G7 Summit was held in Biarritz, France, but there was no joint communiqué. This is the first time after 44 years that the seven economic powers met in 1975. Many conflicts in this world are caused by our basic 'Human Greed', and we have to deal with these problems together.

There are also chronic environmental degradations globally. Those problems are also due to human greed. Just this year alone, there were 75,000 fires in the Amazon area in South America. It may be far from you, but that precious place is actually the 'Lung of our Planet Earth'.

As we are meeting in Mongolia to come up with new solutions for humanity, we need new solutions to overcome the post-modern civilizational crises. Please look at Lumbini, the birthplace of Sakyamuni Buddha, and the new master vision plan called **Lumbini Vishwa Shanti Nagrama** – a humble place where people can come to live together in environmental soundness and harmony. Every UN Secretary-General has visited this UNESCO heritage area – citing Lumbini as "A Place of Significant Human Value".

After working on Lumbini for more than 15 years with the people in Nepal and world Buddhist communities, I am more than happy to explain to

Kwaak Young-hoon, Associate Professor of Decision Sciences, The George Washington University School of Business, U.S.A.

you about the vision and how to build this Lumbini, P.H.D., Peace and Harmony District. With all your joint effort, we will realize this new city of 24-km by 24-km in Nepal – a beautiful country of "Never Ending Peace and Love".

French President Macron announced at this G7 Summit to immediately raise 20 million euros to support the Brazilian government in preventing fire in the Amazon area. That is a good start. I hope that after our Samvad III Dialogue here in Ulaanbaatar, we will come up with a Resolution to raise even more seed money from all nations to start building the city infrastructure for Lumbini – ultimately, a place for all the people of the World.

1. Overview

The legend of Siddhartha Gautama Sakyamuni Buddha began in Lumbini nearly 2,600 years ago, and his teaching is embraced by millions of Buddhists around the world. However, Lumbini – the birthplace of Sakyamuni Buddha – has been ignored for too long, and many people lamented the present undeveloped and poor living conditions in this sacred place.

At this juncture of human history, when our world is in constant crisis, some visionaries begin to see that this obscured Lumbini – the birthplace of Buddha – can evolve to become a living and learning spiritual place, a fountain of world peace that will bring hope to this troubled world.

A Brief Background and Recent History

In December 1998, the World Buddhist Summit was held in Lumbini, and it was declared that Lumbini is "the Holiest Buddhist Pilgrimage Center of Buddhists and Peace-loving People of the World," and the "*Fountain of World Peace.*" This was a major change in the general perception of Lumbini and a chance to develop its true potential.

Immediately after the Declaration, several Buddhist leaders and Dr. H. Karcher of UNDP in Kathmandu set the overall strategy for the development of Lumbini as the Fountain of World Peace. The defined task was divided into three phases: "(1) *the vision and scoping phase,* (2) *the operation study phase and* (3) *the implementation phase*".

In November 1999, the United Nations in New York and UNDP in Kathmandu commissioned Dr Kwaak Young-hoon of Harvard Divinity School in Boston and Dr Abelardo Brenes of UN University for Peace in Costa Rica to carry out the *Vision and Scoping Phase* with the purpose of "...scoping the development of Lumbini beyond the physical infrastructure and economic development envisaged in the Lumbini plan developed in the 1970s.

In May 2000, after making field visits and discussing with the World Fellowship of Buddhists as well as representatives of governments, Dr Kwaak and Dr Brenes recommended Lumbini as a World Peace City where Buddhists and citizens of the world "live to learn to live together," and "propagate their practical learning to the rest of the world."

In December 2004, at the 2nd World Buddhist Summit held in Lumbini, the recommendation in the May 2000 *Mission Report for the Vision and Scoping of Lumbini as World Peace City* was unanimously adopted.

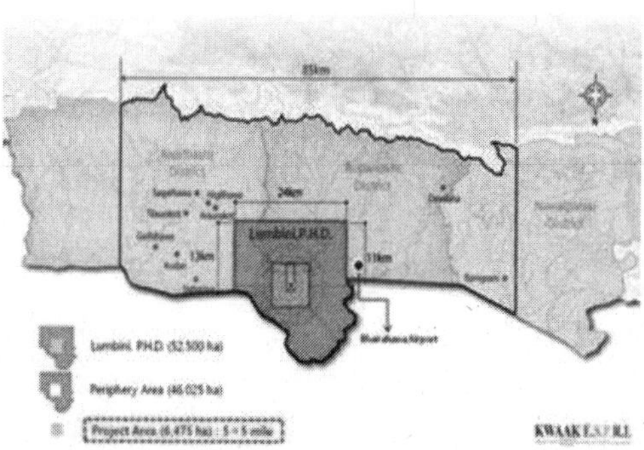

Lumbini, P.H.D. (Peace and Harmony District)

The Kwaak-Brenes *Mission* in 2000 also recommended that the Government of Nepal take immediate action to enter into the second phase to "Operationalize the Lumbini Vision and Scoping Report". After 12 years of passing **KWAAK E.S.P.R.I., Environmental Studies and Policy Research Institute** from Seoul, Korea, was ultimately commissioned by the Governments of Nepal and Korea in March 2012 to prepare a *"Master Vision Plan for Lumbini World Peace City Preservation and Development."*

2. Project Purpose and Design Principles

We learned from many peace-loving people in the world, including Buddhist leaders and Lumbini villagers, that making Lumbini, this very birthplace of Buddha, as Vishwa Shanti Nagrama is an *unprecedented rare opportunity to contribute to humanity and it should not be missed.* They urged us to highlight the noble purposes of Lumbini and to demonstrate how our human environment can be conceived and orchestrated to integrate both rural and urban lifestyles and to help facilitate the evolution of Global Village Civilization to be more harmonious and just.

KWAAK E.S.P.R.I. organized what we learned from the stakeholders of Lumbini consisting of local residents, government officials, scholars and high monks, and turned their teachings, hopes and dreams into **four project purposes and design principles** for Lumbini Vishwa Shanti Nagrama as follows:

1) Preserve and protect the historical, cultural, religious and ecological treasures of the area.
   Immediate actions must be taken to safeguard Lumbini from irreversible damage.
   - "No house should be involuntarily removed."
   - "No archaeological sites should be disturbed."
   - "No more polluting industrialization and urban sprawl."
   - "No more deforestation and Restore the forest."
2) Embody the principles in practical application of the three treasures of Buddhism
   - "Buddha, Dharma and Sangha are to be spatially laid out."
   - "Lotus should be symbolized."
   - "8 Truth Paths should be introduced."
3) Provide a living and learning environmental model conducive to self-enlightenment and to the formation of a more harmonious Global Village Civilization.

- "Upasaka/Upasika, a concept for world citizens, should be introduced."
- "Provide additional new rural villages for new incoming farmers."

4) Alleviate poverty and improve the quality of life in rural villages in the greater Lumbini area.
   - "Peace cannot come amidst hunger and disease."
   - "Economic and ecological sustainability should be ensured."
   - "At every level of implementation, local residents must be involved, and human development must be considered."

3. Planning Philosophy and Physical Layout Design

KWAAK E.S.P.R.I. has been practising for the last 45 years with the six environmental viewpoints: (1) spatial-physical environment, (2) economic-social environment, (3) eco-natural environment, (4) historical-cultural environment, (5) aesthetic-visual environment, and (6) mind-spiritual environment. With these six viewpoints, some questions about the city's environmental design have arisen.

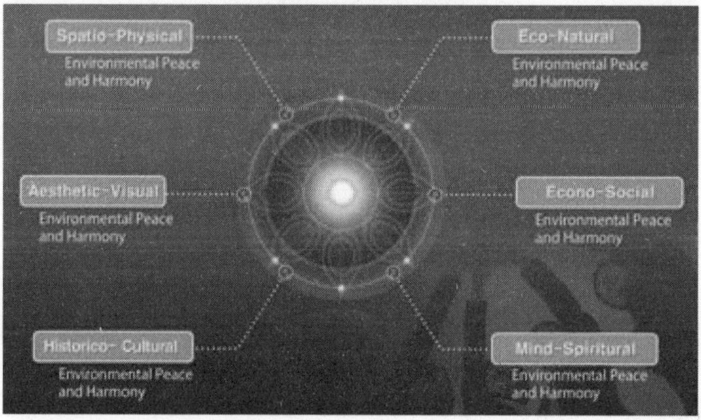

How could the relationship between the form of Lotus and the functions of the Buddhist 3 Treasures and 8 Truth Paths coincide? What do we do with the 1.6km × 1.6km Sacred Garden in the South and with the LDT area of 1.6km × 4.8km in relation to the advice? How best to allocate the projected population of 220,000 in the target year 2030 for the 8km × 8km and half a million for the *Lumbini, P.H.D.* If it comes to one million, what do you do? I will explain the plan concept.

1. The first planning decision was that the Sacred Garden should be in the center of *Lumbini, P.H.D.*, Vishwa Shanti Nagrama, with the

existing 1.6km × 1.6km area, and our plan should provide more protection for the Sacred Garden, especially all three sides of the Southern, Eastern, and Western boundaries of the Sacred Garden. The Sacred Garden, with a diameter of 1.6km, has been designated forever as the *Buddha Zone.*

2. The *Dharma Zone* was created right outside the Buddha Zone, the largest Dharma Wheel in the world, with a 3.2km diameter and a width of 0.8km. On the outer side of a 1.4km radius, in the rim of the Dharma Wheel with 200m in width, KWAAK E.S.P.R.I. allocated the *world citizens university* where institutes of Dharma learning and research centres of excellence in the world can be established. In this Dharma Zone, we should offer a natural forest setting, mainly with Sal trees, for peaceful meditation in the original nature of Buddha's time. Pilgrims can rest in this natural forest before entering the Buddha Zone and the Sacred Garden.
3. The *Sangha Zone* is laid at the 1.6km outer side of the Dharma Zone. Seven new Sanghas are arranged around the Dharma Wheel and together with the present LDT management area to make the perfect Lotus flower with eight petals.

   With this land use pattern, KWAAK E.S.P.R.I. satisfied all **3 Treasures** of Buddhism. No commercial hotels will be allowed, but only Guest Houses run by residents. We planned the Guest Houses in every Neighbour Family Unit in the Sanghas based on the Nepalese tradition of "Atithi Devo Bhava." This way, economic benefits stay within the Sanghas, and more than anything, long-term visitors and pilgrims will be able to live with residents and learn about their way of life. Buddhist leaders also made it clear that in these three inner zones, no meat is to be consumed.
4. Another design decision is to introduce the idea of inviting peace-loving world citizens to live in *Lumbini, P.H.D.,* Vishwa Shanti Nagrama; that is, the provision of *Upasaka/ Upasika Zone and New Rural Village Zone.* They are introduced *outside* of the Sangha Zone. These Zones are sub-divided into *108 land parcels* where global participations are encouraged. Peace-loving people from all over the world can build their own architectural styles of houses and neighbourhoods but with *two strict conditions:* one is to build with their best ecologically sustainable and the other is the best neighbourhood example of living together in harmony in their own cultures.

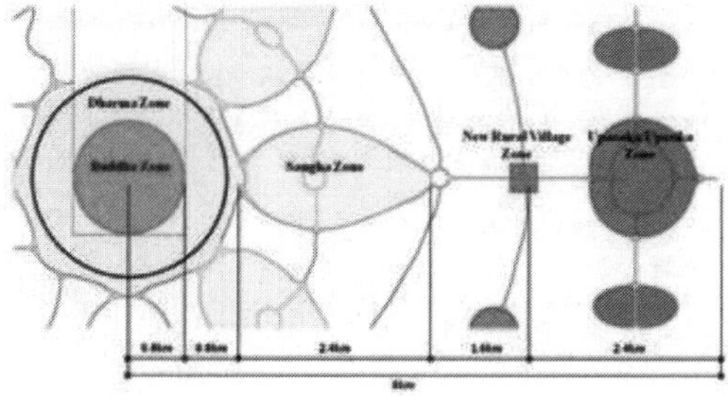

Lumbini Vishwa Shanti Nagrama

Buddha	Dharma	Sangha	New Rural-Village, Upasaka/Upasika
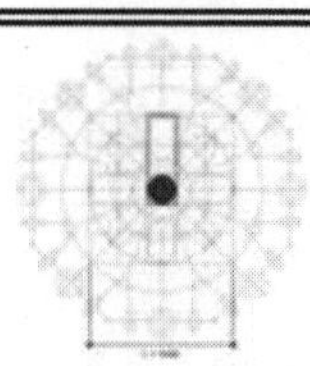	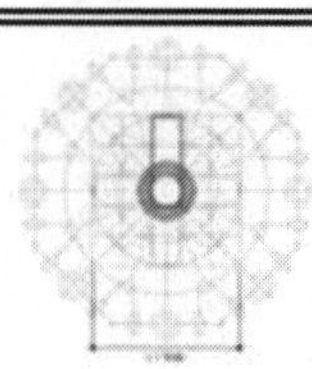	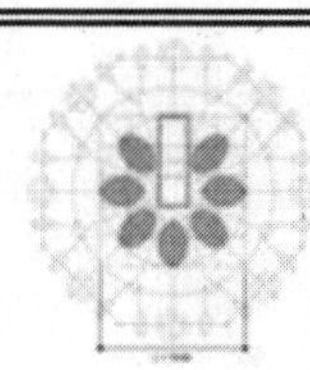	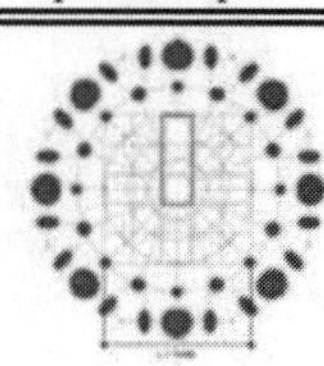

After extensive transportation and circulation system analysis, we introduced the ring road for the periphery of Upasaka/Upasikas.

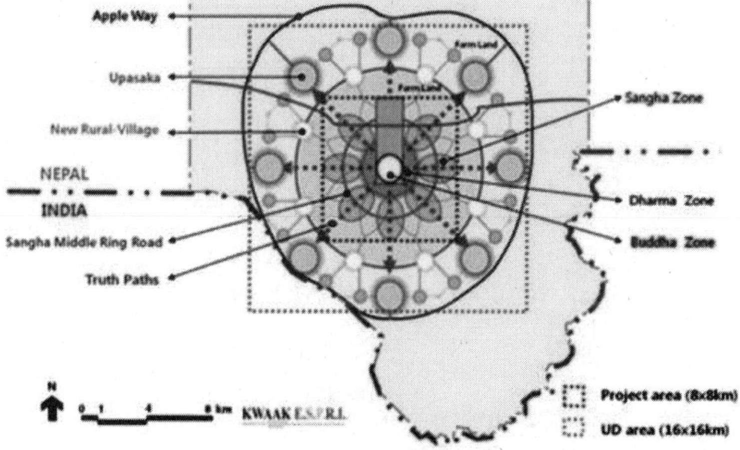

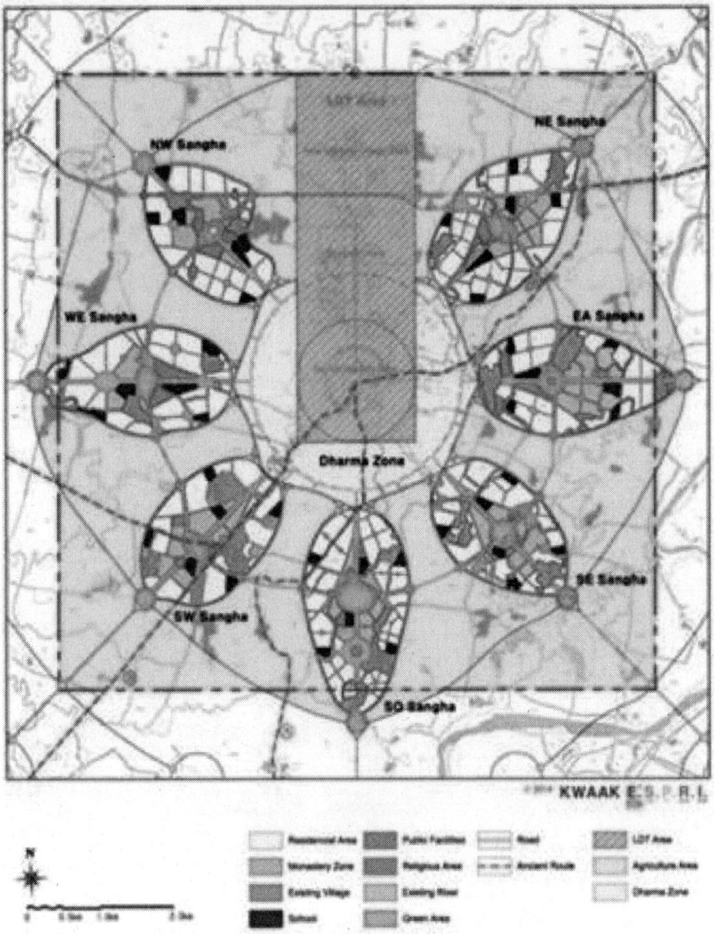

Sangha Zone Land Use Plan

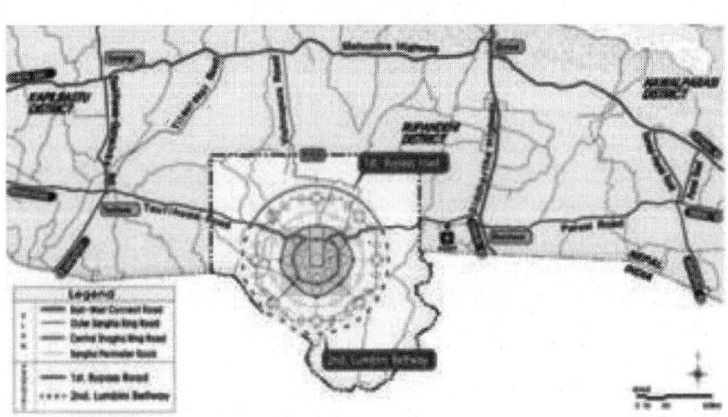

Regional Road System

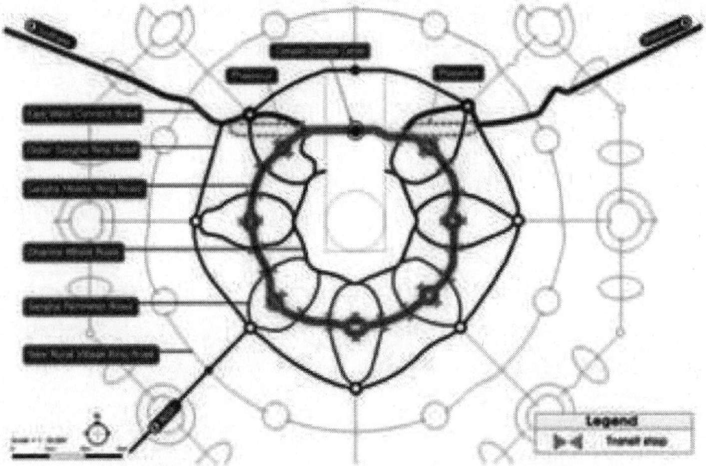

Inner Traffic System and Sangha Middle Ring Public Transit

4. Implementation Plan

In the past, wealthy nations or charities usually donated money and resources to programs for the developing countries and may send aid workers to oversee these projects. Today, more pro-active and integrated partnerships and "hands-on" teaming relationships have emerged between nations.

Therefore, the Nepal's Government should engage the developed countries, worldwide Buddhist groups and private foundations who recognize the value of *Lumbini, P.H.D.* as a "humanistic project" of the highest order. In order to succeed, all levels of Nepal Government and Buddhists groups must actively partner with the donor groups and participate from the initial planning stage to the final construction.

After a critical assessment of the financing, phasing and marketing aspect, KWAAK E.S.P.R.I. laid out a strategic plan to secure potential governmental subsidies plus public and private funding that can help realize *Lumbini, P.H.D.* Master Vision Plan.

Lumbini, P.H.D. Implementation Strategy will include the following funding sources and fund-raising methods:

- Partnership with all of the ODA countries in terms of matching funds to the future land tenure from the 7 Sanghas and the 108 land parcels of the Upasaka/Upasika Zone.

- Encourage active participations from global Buddhist organizations, foundations, individual Buddhists and all peace-loving people in the world.
- Seed money from public funding and Private donations.
- Donations from pilgrims.

Lumbini, P.H.D. is to be developed in an orderly manner based on the Master Vision Plan. No residential or rural agricultural lands will be allowed to develop or build on their own without the timely approval and careful monitoring of *Lumbini, P.H.D. Commission* which is to be set up with full legal authorities to use the funds to execute the Master Vision Plan.

Special Laws for Lumbini, P.H.D. Commission: Special new laws for a public body to execute *Lumbini, P.H.D.* should be enacted to deal with the transparent management of the land acquisition, design and construction programs, religious promotion, pilgrimage organization, concessionaire supports and financial accounting, all of which answering to the Nepalese government and the public.

5. Conclusion

The 21st Century confronts an ultimatum from our planet for its future well-being. Lumbini is positioned to become one of the pioneer spiritual communities to face this environmental threat and human sufferings. It is time to seize this opportunity to implement *Lumbini, P.H.D.* as the Fountain of World Peace and as *an epoch-making historical model of spirituality.*

Lumbini, P.H.D. was, therefore, orchestrated for humanity coming through the 8 Truth Paths through Sanghas and 8 more Truth Paths through rural open space from every parts of the world to participate in the development of Upasaka/Upasika and New Rural Villages and for their progress in a sustainable manner, integrating both rural and urban lifestyles, and facilitating a new "modus vivendi" of living together. In *Lumbini, P.H.D.*, there will be no air, water and noise pollutions. There will be no place where learning and living Dharma of Shanti, Bandhutwa, Maitri and Sadbhav can be avoided.

I wish all of us in this 2019 Ulan Bator occasion decide and declare today that every peace-loving people on Planet Earth is invited to join hands-in hands and to build step-by-step together *Lumbini, P.H.D., Global Villagers' World Peace City* to resolve avoidance of conflict and environment degradation all together!

We have been talking for the past 2500 years. Let's do it now! It is the Ulaanbaatar Ultimatum!

The Kathmandu Post" December 7, 2012

10

M. Zolzaya

Abstract: *National values are generally people's collective intellectual solidarity. Examples of national values are independence, peace, security, traditional culture and native language. Author analyzed on the sociological research was titled "Mongolians' values" (2018) of Mongolian State University of Culture and Arts. This research included 1500 respondents of 11 aimags and capital.*

National values system explained their culture to accordance with the human's values. In the global age, countries are defining self-values as part of their unique heritage. In recent years, Mongolian researchers conducted some research regard to this theme. For example, researchers of University of Finance and Economics included about 4000 respondents in 2015. In 2017, The Management Academy included 797 respondents in the sociological survey titled "Defining the Mongolians values by the Schwartz theory of basic values".[1]

In axiology, values are divided into its characters. For example, abstract and concrete; material and intellectual; ethics, aesthetics, religion and legal; absolutely and relatively; for the genealogy, primary and secondary etc. [2] General classifications of values – intellectual and material – are recognized in both Marxism and broader axiological theories.. In generally, it includes the science, knowledge, rational elements and emotional things in intellectual values.

For Germany philosopher Max Scheler, a value divided emotive, life, intellectual (beauty, ethics, and epistemology) and religious into sphere of value-phenomena.[3] American philosopher W.K. Frankena consider that a value

M. Zolzaya, Head of Department of Cultural Studies, Institute of Arts and Culture, Mongolian State University of Culture and Arts, Mongolia.

"power values of effort, freedom, lucky, and novity contributed by art, music and personal judgement, which appear in moment of the freedom".[4] H. Reiner classified "Objective beneficial values do not depend on the need of subject, individual character, values of subject are subjective values".[5] These classifications depends on the content of that research. Most nationalities agree that intellectual values like independence, solidarity, and sovereignty are vital, as they are shaped by history, cultural heritage, native language, religion, and identity.

National values became their intellectual sense direction and beliefs of this people. Particularly, culture define national values, which became their identity. Therefore, National Security Concept of Mongolia (S.3) makes "The foundation for ensuring national security, unity and consensus shall rest on good social morality, sound social psychology and shared social values." and "The State, citizens and mass media shall jointly implement a policy to shape a social psychology in accordance with which citizens will be proud of their country, nationality, national accomplishments and progress and respect national interests, ethics, law and statehood".

Mongolian State University of Arts and Culture conducted titled "*Mongolians values*" (2018) of Mongolian State University of Culture and Arts. This research included 1500 respondents of 11 aimags and Ulaanbaatar capital in 2018. The Goals of this sociological research are: To define current mongolians value and their values trend. Every person can understand other value.

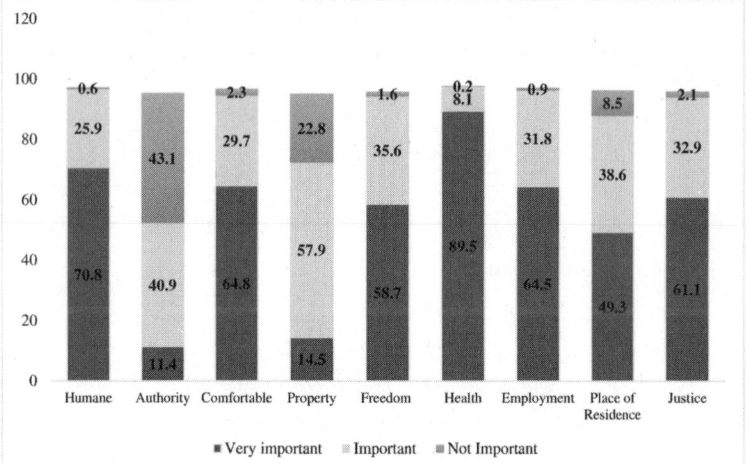

Figure 1: The most important things in good life

When asked very important values of respondents for their living good life, 89.5 per cent named health, humanity 70.8 per cent, comfortable 64.8 per cent, employment 64.5 per cent, justice 61.1 per cent, freedom 58.7 per cent, place of residence 49.3 per cent, and property 72.4 per cent, 43.1 per cent expressed authority is not important. From comprehension, life needs of person answered that material property is most important.

For respondents, moral values are justice (16.2 per cent), responsibilities (15.2 per cent), humanity (14.4 per cent), patriotism (9.8 per cent), good (9.7 per cent), kindness (8.2 per cent), good name (7.6 per cent), collective (6.5 per cent), happiness (6.2 per cent), and companionship (6.1 per cent). Respondents answered that justice is highly important in moral values. Since, "What does justice mean to you?" 36.4 per cent equality, 18.1 per cent to living according to common law, 14.8 per cent moral standards, and 14.2 per cent loyality.

The majority respondents respect health, family and knowledge. Figure 2 suggests that 25.6 per cent of respondents (25.6 per cent) think most important for health of family members, 17.2 per cent children, 16.4 per cent to care for parents, 14.9 per cent love, 14.0 per cent trust, 10.2 per cent lineage, 1.0 per cent home divinity and 0.4 per cent inheriting property from predecessor. Here, most important factors that they consider family climate. A few of them answered that one of the family values are home divinity and inheriting property from predecessor.

In Mongolian traditional teaching express, the most important children's moral education more than inheriting property.

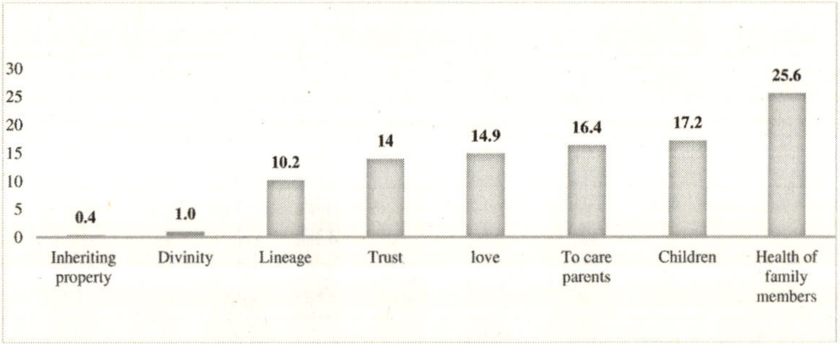

Figure 2: What is your family values?

We formulated the Mongolian National values system that **moral** (solidarity, patriotism, collective idea; justice, responsibilities and rules;

compassion, human qualities), **political** (independent, national fundamental interests; democracy, freedom and, equability; respecting state, theory of the "two principles" (the order of the religion – *nom-un yosun*, the order of the state-*törö-yin yosun*), **arts** (national arts; public arts; classical arts), **religious** (traditional religion; tolerant of the beliefs of others; freedom of religion), **cultural** (cultural heritage; national culture, custom and rite; culture of personal, organization, public), and **economics** (market economy; natural resource, ecosystem; creative labour).

Largest number of respondents answered that agreed our formulation. These values system contain national and humanity values.

For S. Tsedendamba, *"In our society increased trends and interest of religion, it is attracting attention the co-ordinates of some opposing interests. Generally people need necessary beliefs. I might be feel more the need of belief in the open society. It prevailing trend as people are trending to religion in level of normal conscious"*.[6] So, we need include phenomena of religion value to intellectual values.

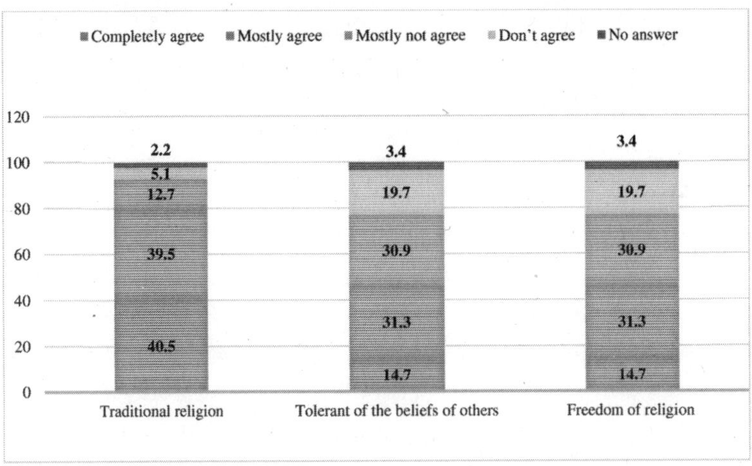

Figure 3: Religious values

Among the majority of respondents agreed traditional religion including in the religious value. Our National Security Concept of Mongolia (S.3.) makes as "Traditional Buddhist...". Which is being used in our research is a this term. And they dealed with unpleasent for tolerant of the beliefs of others; freedom of religion. People have not too much sufficient understanding on the freedom of religion, so who ought maximise support for training freedom of religion for the masses.

Buddhist religion express basis characters of Mongolian civilization, keeper and transmitter history and culture, motivator the restoration of national consciousness, stabilizing social life, new religious movements put into our life, to screen and to protect from foreign cultural power[7].

One of the political values is two principles transmitted by Buddhism. It is viewed the theory of the "two principles" [mong. Khoyar yosun], religion and state.

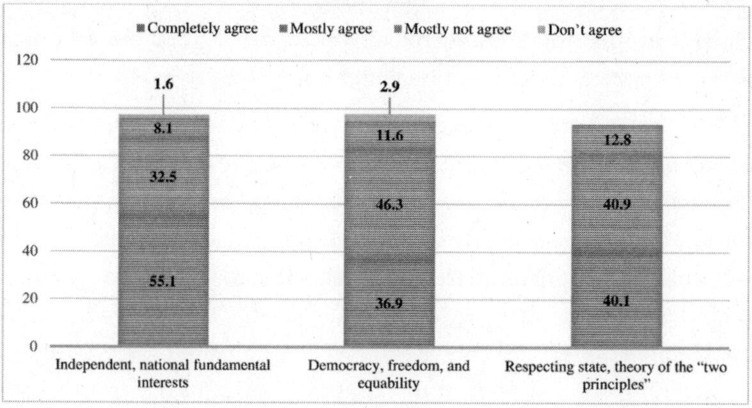

Figure 4: Political values

State Policy of Mongol Yuan Dynasty the "two principles" in political value sphere now. Scholar Sh. Choimaa defined that Mongol queens started study two principles from *Ögedei* Khan's third son Koden (1206-1251) period,[8] *"It is moral education programme of queens, lord, officials, monks and commoners. Other words, this principle teaches us how to purify from evils and virtue of the body, language, and mind."* Academician J.Boldbaatar *"nom-un turu was ideology of buddhist religion, but state should respect mental and learned man should work in public service, if, state had revised by religion."*[9] Other hand, religion is phenomen of cultural value.

We are including traditional custom, tangible and intangible cultural heritage, organizational and public culture in cultural values.

In here, we regarding more understandable to respondents term of 5 types of social consciousness in classic social philosophy. According to results, 59.5 per cent of respondents answered that political consciousness is weak, 53.5 per cent of them moral consciousness is too weak. 43.1 per cent of them answered that religious consciousness has average evaluation.

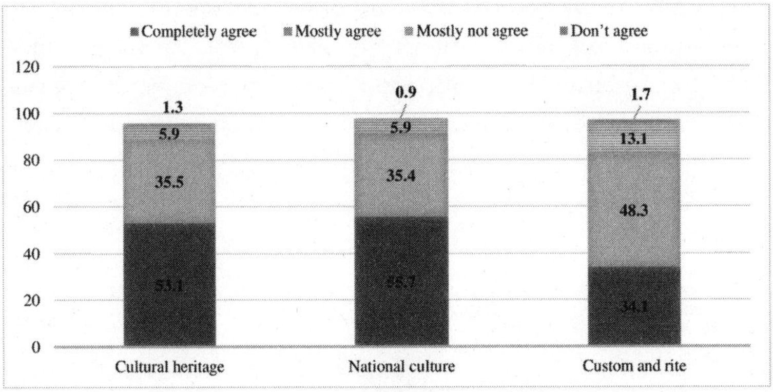

Figure 5: Cultural values

The largest numbers of respondents chose relatively positive opinion on individual and national values. There have quite in contrast between values formation on the society and person respecting values, which determined with socioeconomic and intelligence factors. In other word, respondents named their high values in research, and they think that should be left always values in their life. They answered that the environment were not too much satisfactory.

We asked more influence family education, education, social environment, and knowledge for formation of a person. Thus, to increase of parents' responsibility, show an example with Mongol culture, tradition and values of humanity are very important key factors.

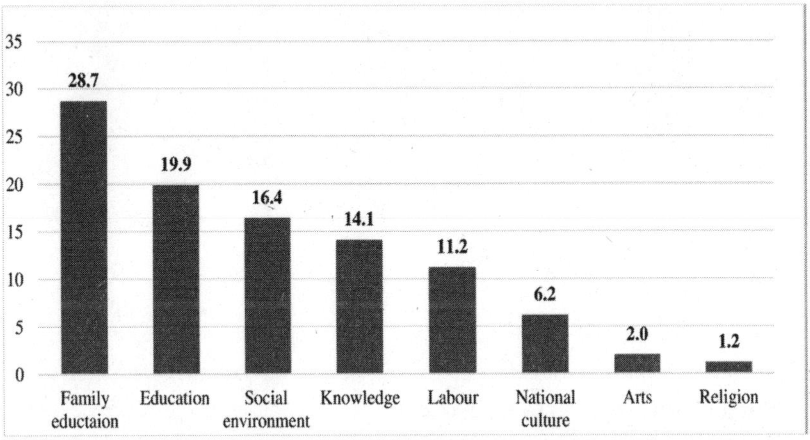

Figure 6: What influences positive factors to education and formation?

The family traditional education and personal development determined by an individual wishes, education, and learn national culture, which can influence to children and their formation. In quantative research, respondents undervalued the roles of religious education, but experts of qualitive research said that organizations of Buddhist religion should toward to a social enlightenment and philanthropy activities in society. As well as the teaching of Buddhist religion always teaches for mind peace of people.

"The religion is very highly value. Religion instinct always exist in the human brain...".

"Mongolians' values" sociological survey.
Focus group interview. Male. Academician.

Focus group interviewer said if that when childhood could be introduce the nature of Buddhist religion, it can influence their during one's lifetime education.

...Buddhist religion teaches nature of inner mind. Generally, how to tame mind.

"Mongolians' values" sociological research.
Focus group interview. Male. Teacher.

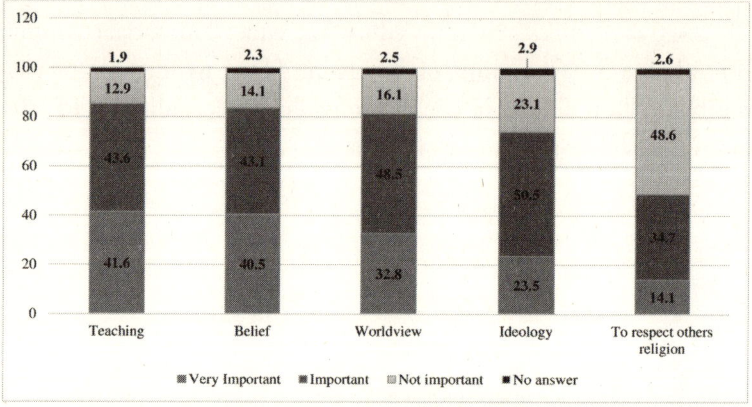

Figure 7: What is your religion values?

Next main question is religious value. Largest of respondents preferred the religious teaching, beliefs and worldview, over 50 per cent don't exact spreading many religions in our country.

In 2008, Institute of Culture and Arts titled "Cultural service to human development" conducted among 4406 respondents of Mongolian 21 aimags.

71.3 per cent of them believe Buddhist religion, 4.3 per cent Christian religion, 4.1 per cent Muslim religion, 1.9 per cent shamanism, 18.3 per cent atheist and, 1.0 per cent other.[10] Institute of Philosophy, Sociology and Law conducted titled "Youth's life purpose, values change" (2010). 81.2 per cent of youth aged 16-35 believe Buddhist religion. 64.1 per cent of them reason for religious belief is since their ancestors having believed Buddhist religion. And 11.8 per cent answered that religion gives me faith and support in life; 42.3 per cent that I meet with lamas, astrologists, and traditional practitioners; 25.5 per cent almost never only if absolutely necessary; 15.1 per cent don`t believe in lamas, astrologists, and traditional practitioners. When ask on youth`s protect traditional religion, 52.7 per cent answered traditional religion is part of the culture and therefore it is necessary to protect; 16.6 per cent traditional religion is more correct and, therefore, it should be protected; 19 per cent of them answered because many religions are spreading into the country, and not necessary to limited to traditional religion.[11]

For some, Buddhism is a religion. For others, it is a philosophy, while others practice Buddhism to find themselves and experience inner peace. Buddhism is a religion that is practiced worldwide. In fact, it is believed that as many as 535 million people around the world practice this religion, which would represent between 8 per cent and 10 per cent of the world's total population.[12] Also results of other research and statistics in Mongolia shows our country that have a mostly proportion of Buddhist religious followers.

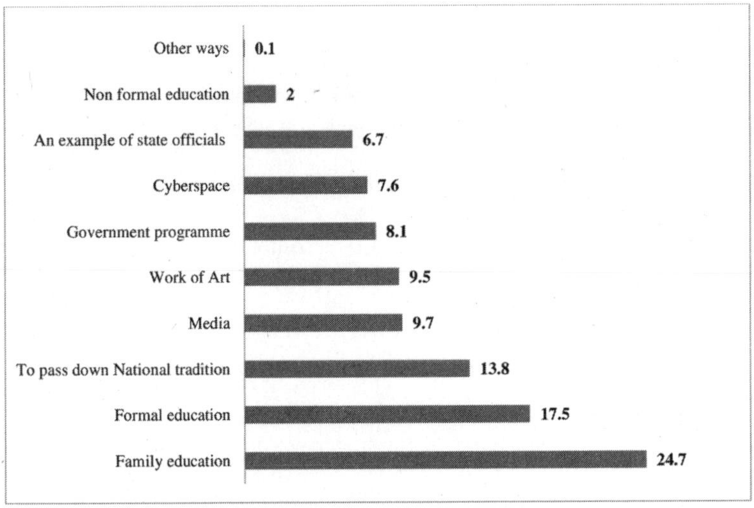

Figure 8: What is the best way to educate value for children and youths?

Respondents of "*Mongolians values*" survey, that would like use family education, formal education, National tradition and Media for children and youngers` education. So, we should to inform the nature and teaching of Buddhist religion by useful version for people.

Largest respondents of the "*Mongolians' values*" survey viewed that justice, solidarity, humanity, patriotism, responsibility and co-operation are of moral values. And experts of qualitive research influencing Globalization, westernization, foreign culture, spreading of many religious are external factors to current Mongols' values change. In future, we ought to support stability of intellectual values in our society. It should reflect importance as be tolerant others` religions and cultures for National cultural values be integrated with the values of humanity. So, we should to inform the nature and teaching of Buddhist religion by useful version for people.

NOTES

1. Defining the Mongolians Values by the Schwartz Theory of Basic Values, Survey Report, UB, 2017.
2. Анисимов С.Ф. Введение в аксиологию. М., 2001. с. 75, in Russian.
3. Max Scheler, *Formalism in Ethics and Non-Formal Ethics of Values*, Trans by Manfred Frings and Robert Funk, Evanston: Northwestern University Press, 1973.
4. Frankena W.K., *Ethics*, N.Y. Prentice Hall, 1963.
5. Reiner H. Die Philosophische Ethik, *Die Fragen und Lehrer in Geschichte und Gegenwart.* Heidelberg, 1964.
6. 'Reform of Mongolian Society', MAS, IP, UB, 2013, p. 138.
7. Ibid., p. 142.
8. *Чоймаа Ш. Хос ёсны сургаалаар төрөө засаж ирсэн уламжлал.* //https://www.sinoss.net/qikan/uploadfile/2010/1130/9759.pdf. 2019.08.29.
9. *Boldbaatar J. Khubilai Khan's Policy,* Khubilai khaan and Mongolian Yuan Dinesty, UB, 2015, p. 42.
10. 'Purev Ts. Cultural Service to Human Development', *Philosophy and Legality Studies*, Vol. XXIII, UB, 2008.
11. 'Mongolian youths' Social Image IPSL', MAS, Ulaanbaatar, 2012.
12. http://worldpopulationreview.com/countries/buddhist-countries/.

11

SHOKO MEKATA

Good afternoon, everyone. I am very grateful to participate in this symposium as one of the speakers. First, I would like to thank the organizers, Vivekananda International Foundation, Gandan Tegchenling Monastery, Mongolia and the Institute of Strategic Studies of the National Security Council of Mongolia. Especially, the Vivekananda International Foundation gave me this great opportunity. Also, many people in Japan helped me too. Thank you very much.

My talk today is on "Shared Values and Democracy in Asia." The term and the concept of "democracy" originally came from the Western world to Asia during the pre-modern era, and we are still seeing that "democracy" in Asia is growing and developing in unique ways. When we talk about something such as "democracy," we often mention something which has happened recently or happens now, or, might happen in the future. So, in the opposite direction, today, I would like to focus on something related to democratic values from the past. There is an old book written in the Tibetan language which talks about morality and knowledge based on Buddhist thinking. The book has many good examples of morality, which are connected to the concept of "shared values" from the Buddhist point of view. We could learn many things from the book regarding "shared values," not just for following the Buddhist way but for something more universal.

The book is named "A Treasury of Elegant Sayings," written in Tibetan in the 13th century by a famous Tibetan scholar, Sakya Pandita Kunga Gyeltsen (Sa skya pandita Kun dga' rgyal mtshan, 1182–1251). He was born in a noble family in Central Tibet in the 12th century and became a monk and a famous

Shoko Mekata, Department of South Asian Studies, Harvard University, U.S.A.

scholar. He went to a Mongol palace, which is currently in Lan-chou, China, when the Mongolian prince summoned him. He wrote very many books, and five of them are especially famous in the Tibetan world. One of them is the book "A Treasury of Elegant Sayings." There are nine chapters and 457 verses in the book, and each verse tells a moral lesson based on Buddhist teachings or thinking. Sakya Pandita wrote this treatise with simple words with many similes and metaphors so that common people could understand easily. Also, he wrote the book influenced by the famous Indian scholar, Nagarjuna, who was born in the 2nd century. This book was translated into Mongolian quite soon after it was written, probably in the late 13th century or the early 14th century. It is still very popular in both Tibet and Mongolia.

Now, I would like to talk a little bit about my personal experience learning from this text. The first time I read the book in Tibetan was with my Tibetan teacher, Prof. Khangkar Tshultim Kesang (Khang dkar Tshul khrims bskal bzang), when I was an undergrad student in Japan. My teacher was born in Western Tibet and came to Japan later in life. He has been teaching many people, and I am one of them. I took some of his courses, including a course on this book, "A Treasury of Elegant Sayings," while I was at my university because I was interested in Tibetan Buddhism, history and culture. That's why I proceeded to study Tibetan studies in graduate school and received my Ph.D. in Tibetan history. So, I am very thankful to my teacher for being able to speak at this symposium today about a verse by Sakya Pandita.

Now, I would like to read a verse by Sakya Pandita from "A Treasury of Elegant Sayings."

Those who have little understanding separate (people) saying
'This is a friend; this is an enemy
Those who have excellent understanding are kind to all
Because it is not certain who will be of benefit

This verse means that people who have compassion treat other people equally. When we see people, we usually recognize those people based on their looks, ways of talking, where they are from, or what kind of religion they believe in. This is a kind of normal behaviour for us because we really do not have much information for judging those people when we see them for the first time. But also, as you know, that is very risky, too. I understand that some people who have some kind of special sense can see through people's nature, but most of us cannot not do that. I, myself, sometimes have the experience of discovering new sides of a person that I never realized were there or even seeing that someone's character is the opposite of how it first appears.

When I was living somewhere in a foreign country in Asia, I used to go to a store near my place. A lady who was working at the store seemed very unfriendly to everyone, and many of my friends told me that she was always very rude. I felt the same way the first time I met her. But I tried to say to her things like "hello," "thank you," and "goodbye" every time when I saw her since I often went to the store. Then she started smiling at me sometimes. And gradually, she began to smile and say "hello" and "thank you" to me, and she even tried to take care of me more. For example, one time, she opened the popsicle package for me when I bought it, probably because I did not speak her language, so she must have thought I really could not do many things just like a child, even opening the package of the popsicle. Actually, not just this lady but also many other people in that place were becoming much kinder to me after I tried to be nice to them. Some of my friends said that most of the people in that country were just not so nice to people, that that was just their culture. I suppose that might be true in some ways. But I thought it was very difficult or impossible to guess the value of culture from another culture's point of view, because of the differences between cultures. Then, I learned that it was very important to do something nice from one's effort, even if it did not seem to benefit me. It is important for me to do something nice or right even if I am not sure that will change the situation.

I currently live in America. I sometimes return to Japan to see my family and visit other countries. Also, I have friends from many different countries. There are many kinds of people around me, and I really enjoy having conversations or sharing life with them. In America, of course it depends on people and places, and I sometimes feel that people do not understand other people who have different values from them. It is often impossible to accept different values from one's own since each person believes in certain values. But it is very important to recognize that other people might have different values from one's own, even though we really do not understand them. This is the point of the verse from the Tibetan scholar Sakya Pandita, which I quoted earlier. That is exactly how many countries have developed in terms of religions and history, such as India and Japan, my country. We Japanese have been keeping and developing some religions such as Shinto, Buddhism, Christianity, and so forth. Of course, there have been many conflicts between these religions in the course of history. Irrespective of that we have a history in which they have been coexisting for a long time. This is the situation not just in Japan or India but also in many other countries in Asia.

In the Western world, historically, not always but often, one side has been an absolute authority, and others are considered as just something evil. And that kind of thinking sometimes has made it very difficult for different sets of values to coexist in peace. In my understanding, "shared values" does not mean that we need to share the same values, but that we know that there are different sets of values in Asia and that we should encourage mutual understanding and sharing of some values for our future in Asia. Historically, many places or countries in Asia have done that before. That is a unique characteristic phenomenon in Asia, I believe. And that is exactly what some Buddhist scholars such as Sakya pandita suggested more than eight hundred years ago in his writing based on Buddhist thinking.

Some say history is just for learning about previous occurrences, but I do not think that is true. Learning history is for thinking about our present and future, and that gives us some ways to consider the shared values we want for our future.

12

Tenzin Lekshey

When we speak about being environmentally conscious, it is important to understand that human evolution itself has largely been shaped by the confluence of the environment and human activities over centuries. We who are presently living in this world of Y2K proclaim to be the guardian of the world. His Holiness the Dalai Lama states, "*The earth is not just our environment. The earth is our mother.*" However, the question remains: do we, as human beings, truly strive to preserve our Mother Nature? People of all faiths trust and tend to respect Mother Nature to the highest epitome. However, this respect often remains superficial – an emotional inclination without meaningful action. Now and then, people call for saving Earth with slogans, protests, actions and resolutions. Institutions, corporations, nations and international organisations vouch for environmental conservation of making this planet liveable and sustainable. If we supposedly work in making this world a liveable one, then are we selfish enough of giving priority to the well-being of human beings alone? Are we thinking that human beings can sustain independently, or are we thinking that we can live by exploiting everything for the sake of fulfilling human desire? Human desire is unlimited, and to quench that desire, we push for the exploitation of resources. Exploitation beyond imagination and the need. Since ecosystems function as interconnected entities, with biodiversity intricately linked, it is prudent to look beyond individual desires for a sustainable future.

Over millennia of Human existence, we have maintained a great relationship with the whole ecosystem and have initially adored the sun, moon and all the cosmic elements of Earth as the sole symbol of invocation. We still

---

Tenzin Lekshey, CTA Official Spokesperson/Additional Secretary (International Relations).

do believe in the tradition of praying to Mother Nature. However, we have not yet learnt the importance of nature and forgotten its centrality of existence.

In my homeland, Tibet – the Land of Snow – Tibetans have, for centuries, regarded the land, rivers, mountains, and lakes as sacred. These natural elements remain intrinsic to Tibetan identity. All our mountains, like Most Kailash, Jomo Lhangma, Amnye Machen and Nyenchen Thanglha, are connected to the Tibetan people, and therefore, respect for these mountains and lakes is boundless. With that conviction, we have never exploited our land, which is rich in resources. It remains an untapped pool of resources for centuries. However, in present days, Chinese mining industries are luring in with the hunger to exploit and pollute the sacred land of Tibet.

Though we may have many reasons and excuses for environmental degeneration, I will speak about two factors.

Need versus Want

Human need is measurable and can be of subsistence, but the want is infinite, which is unfathomable. As we understand from Adam Smith's theory of human wants in his 'The Wealth of Nations', it is understandable that the resources are limited, and human wants are unlimited. However, theorists claim to propose effective utilisation of limited resources, but the real world is a crazy world where all yearn for maximum exploitation of resources that deplete our Mother Earth. As Buddhists, we understand that want is tantamount to desire, which is considered poison. It is one of the main causes of suffering that trapped us in the vicious cycle of samsara. Somehow, we do realise that the earth in which we live has an abundant resource to fulfil our needs. Sadly, we become so selfish that we look only for what we want. Therefore, we destroy the earth where we live by digging out more than what we need. In the process, more carbon is emitted into the air, we see drastic changes in the climate pattern. Every year, we experience extreme heat and cold. In Tibet, for example, temperatures are rising at an alarming rate. The average temperature on the Tibetan plateau has climbed 0.43 degrees Celsius per decade – far higher than the global average of 0.12 degrees Celsius per decade.

Nature versus Economy

Every nation, whether capitalist or socialist, believes that they inherit the legitimate rights over using their land, water and air without external interference. Territorial sovereignty at present is at the height of the nation-state discussion. All the powerful countries dictate their rules with the sole objective of complying with the national interest. Priority is the national interest, nothing else. In such circumstances, conflicts and tensions arise. Competition and race are the only ways to succeed rather than cooperation and collaboration. In such a race, we are inclined to overlook the importance of nature by destroying it intentionally and unintentionally.

Since the emergence of the Industrial Revolution, we accelerated the modernisational drive with an unanticipated pace. Now, we have more buildings, towns, cities, and industries than forests, lakes and mountains. Earlier, we used to witness deep forests with plenty of flora and fauna. Now, we have concrete forests with high-rise buildings and motorcars, which contribute largely to carbon emissions. As a fact check, we can state that humans now inhabit only 10 per cent of the world's land, and we built roads, highways, and farmlands with the remaining 80 per cent of the entire land. We can confidently say that humans now inhabit 90 per cent of the world's land, leaving only 10 per cent for wilderness.

Over the years, the economy has been the priority, and in order to build the economy, one neglects and rejects the importance of nature. We have an idea that the environment is important, but we intend to look for prosperity and wealth. We compromise nature with the economy. Those big nations have long understood that the cost of environmental degradation is costly and irreparable. Therefore, they deliberately transport nuclear waste to poorer countries. Such practices of transporting debris of corollary environmental damage are still undergoing. Though many countries are now open to a sustainable or eco-friendly economy, many disasters have been done to nature. Many people understand that the world in which we live has given us a lot, but we treat the world with disgrace. We never thought of complimenting nature for the gift of our life. We snatched many lives and extinct beyond our imagination. With that craze for economy and wealth, we repressed the importance of nature.

What can we do?
Building Environment Conscious

It is difficult to subdue greed, wants and desire. But we can minimise it through different mediums. Different faiths can play a vital role in cultivating human minds with contentment. There is a chain reaction in how much we exploit nature, and the results are not favourable to humankind. We have witnessed it in our lifetime. Floods, droughts, Landslides, Tsunamis, Wildfires, and all the so-called natural (manmade) disasters. If we continue to distort and abuse nature, we will continue to face the havoc of nature. Therefore, it is important to build an understanding of the importance of the environment.

Promotion of Sustainable Development

Priority needs to be put on maintaining sustainable growth and sustainable development. It is the most viable solution for the human race to survive and sustain in the future. Every nation, every corporation, every leader, every civil society and every mass must promote sustainable development. It is a timely and the most rational way of living. This will pave the way for a sustainable future.

I conclude with the words of His Holiness the Dalai Lama: "It is our collective and individual responsibility to preserve and tend to the environment in which we all live." May we all work closely and collectively to preserve the environment – not just for our generation but for future generations to come.

13

ARAYAWANGSO

Buddhism is a universal teaching about the existing normal truth; its principle expounds the ultimate truth as normally present in nature. Buddhism is the natural Dhamma principle which all beings, particularly humankind, should study to understand and realize clearly that this is how things are in nature.

Evam dhammo – It is normally like this;
Evam bhavi – It must be like this;
Evam anatito – It will not change into anything else.

Buddhist Dhamma teaching aims at normality, which is the result that can be regularly observed, with no external influence, and no one can control or command it to be as desired. It can be summed up into the common characteristics as follows:

Sabbe sankhara anicca – all conditioned things are impermanent;
Sabbe sankhara dukkha – all conditioned things are suffering;
Sabbe sankhara anatta – all conditioned things are non-self

Buddhism is not a religion. Neither is it a philosophy, a psychology, a logic, a literature, an art of living, nor a science. However, everything can be considered as one of Buddhism's several dimensions, if it is the truth that does not contradict Dhamma – the principle of normality as truly present in nature.

Buddhism teaches about truth at several levels, aiming toward the ultimate truth, *ariyasacca dhamma* – the most noble truth for life development, for complete extinction of suffering.

Vemerable Arayawangso Phrakhra Paladviriyawat, Buddhapojhariphunchai Forest Monastery, Thailand.
English translation by Dr. Pawadee Tonguthai.

Before entering the first of His 45 years as the Fully Enlightened One, Lord Buddha promulgated the principle of truth for true extinction of suffering, called the **Four Noble Truths** (*ariyasacca* 4) at Isipattana Deer Park, near the town of Varanasi.

The Dhamma teaching is generally recognized under the name of "***Dhammacakkappavattana Sutta***" or "**Lord Buddha's First Sermon**", proclaiming His Self-Enlightenment.

Dhamma principle, which serves as a representation of Buddhism, is the practice along the **Middle Way** (*majjhima patipada*) or the **Noble Eightfold Path**, summarized into the **Three Trainings**: morality (*sila*), concentration (*samadhi*), and wisdom (*panna*).

The Noble Eightfold Path, or the Middle Way, which proceeds with the cultivation of the **Four Foundation of Mindfulness** (*satipatthana* 4) in accordance with the **Nine Steps of Insight Development** (*vipassana nana*), is the authentic Buddhism or the true Dhamma aiming at deliverance from all sufferings (*nibbana*). It is the **goal of life** for those with the status of human beings who are capable of purifying their minds by relying on themselves.

In the last period of His life, just before entering His final *parinibbana* at *Kusinara, Malla* State, the Blessed One gave the following exhortation to a wandering mendicant (*paribbajaka*) named *Subhadda*:

> "*Any Dhamma-Vinaya that contains ariyamagga – the eight noble dhamma, one will be able to find the stream-enterer (sotapanna), the once-returner (sakadagami), the non-returner (anagami), and the holy one (arahant) within that Dhamma-Vinaya.*
>
> *If those monks practice well and properly in accordance with the eight noble dhamma, the world will never be short of the holy ones.*"

Most significantly, Buddhist teaching emphasizes the reliance on oneself and reliance on Dhamma, as in the Buddha's words proclaimed in ***Attadipa Sutta***:

Attadipa viharatha attasarana anannasarana
Dhammadipa dhammasarana anannasarana

Meaning:

Be an island unto yourself, be your own refuge, there is no other;
Have Dhamma as your island, have Dhamma as your refuge, having no other.

At the heart of Buddhism is conducting one's life by relying on oneself, which means developing oneself to have wisdom, to perform the right effort, and by relying on Dhamma, that is, realizing the truth as exist in nature.

Development of life to make it efficient and capable, having good quality, rightly with Dhamma, and in conformance with nature is, therefore, the study and practice to lead life towards well-being and happiness at all levels until finally attaining the final goal of complete extinction of suffering.

This is in accordance with the Dhamma teaching in the **38 Highest Blessings** (*Mangala Sutta*), which lays out distinctly every step of life development, along with the Dhamma principle demonstrating the Truth (*sacca dhamma*) for all levels of life.

How does one coexist with individuals, society and environment in a way that leads to well-being, happiness, and peace – or what is called "**Conflict-free coexistence with the world**"?

We can find teachings with regard to morals, ethic, and virtue at the mundane level such as life management according to the principle of the sublime states of mind (*brahmavihara dhamma*) or relationships with persons, society, and environment according to the principle of the bases for social solidarity (*sangahavatthu dhamma*).

If we can truly conduct our life by following the principle of *brahmavihara dhamma* (loving-kindness, compassion, sympathetic joy, and equanimity), human society will enjoy peace and happiness. The world we live in will instantly turn into heaven.

Moral, ethic, and virtue that we are yearning for will be immediately revived when beings have true loving-kindness and compassion towards each other.

In other words, moral will reappear when the minds of world beings are filled with loving-kindness and compassion. Peace and happiness will return when metta dhamma is supporting the world.

Buddhist Dhamma principle aims at training and teaching the multitude to have wisdom and be maintained in mindfulness until they can put wisdom to work for the right knowledge, the right view, properly with Dhamma – or what is known as *sammaditthi*.

Sammaditthi – the virtue of wisdom – presides over the eight noble dhamma, being most significant for progressing along the path that will terminate all defilements, which are the major enemy, aiming toward true liberation of beings from suffering.

An immense responsibility for all wise and knowledgeable men in Buddhism is how to endow humanity with **the right view.**

Sammaditthi is having the right view about the truth of Dhamma, even at the level of mundane Dhamma, regarding faith and confidence in the **law of kamma.**

A great benefit will arise if humankind have faith in *kamma* and its consequence, along with knowledge and understanding about the truth of Dhamma, and become confident that all of us are beings that depend on our own actions.

Discussion and explanation about kamma (*kammavadi*) is the mark of Buddhism which makes use of the rule and criteria of kamma to create the cause to match the result. If one needs a good result, a good cause must be created; a bad cause will bring bad result.

The law of kamma displays the truth according to Dhamma that is truly present in nature in order to regulate all beings and keep them under the **natural law** (*dhammaniyama*).

Learning to understand Dhamma as exist in nature, and use that knowledge in one's daily life is the study and practice to develop life towards real benefits and happiness. It is the well-being and happiness derived from nature by realizing the **natural law.**

One will also be able to develop life to be **free of conflict with nature** by understanding the natural truth that all things under the law of nature are constantly changing, known as **impermanency** (*anicca).*

Being attached to them something constant is contrary to the law of nature and will build up pressure on the mind that can become unbearable and lead to **suffering** (*dukkha*).

Dukkha arise according to causes and conditions; when causes and conditions are extinct, *dukkha* is also extinct. There is never any real self – this is called non-self (*anatta*).

Accepting the truth by knowing and understanding the law of nature will make humankind conduct their life in a way that does not create conflict with each other and encourage them to help one another. Dhamma of loving-kindness and compassion will then arise.

World beings will be able to overcome a variety of conflict and harm with *sammaditthi*, which will subsequently guide them to the right thought and right practice, truly proper with moral and ethic.

We should therefore join together in the extensive propagation of the teaching that is truthful – Dhamma principle – for the cultivation of **wisdom and the right view**. This will be the key that can truly unlock the door toward **Peace with Dhamma**.

If humanity is **lacking in wisdom**, **deprived of the right view**, the world will soon face ruin and destruction. Human beings will be overwhelmed by conflicts, both with one another and with the natural environment, bringing about all sorts of natural disaster such as the current global warming crisis that is the consequence of mankind leading their lives with the wrong views.

The time has come to call on the world community, all religions, and all ethnicities to focus on the cultivation of wisdom, to form the right view as properly with the truth that is **Dhamma** as existing in nature.

Sammaditthi – the right view – arising in their minds will guide them along the path of the right practice, in accordance with the *ariyamagga* – the Noble Eightfold Path – as has been presented here.

Blessing with metta.

14

Vinay Sahasrabuddhe

Excellency Minister for Environment and Tourism of the Govt of Mongolia, Mr TSERENBAT Namsrai, venerable religious leaders and thinkers, scholars, academics and other ladies and gentlemen,

It's a privilege to be invited here to address this important conference and I am thankful to the organisers for the same!

Social scientists in US are reportedly worried about the fact that millennial generation of their country appears to be thoroughly incapable of ability to empathies. In an atmosphere filled with ultra-individualism, for many in the Western part of the globe, world is not just becoming flat but also becoming more and more small. Many believe that the size of the world is limited to what they are exposed to. Happily, a software engineer in some other part of the world and worried about the lack of ability to empathies applied his creative mind and came out with an idea of a computer game which is known as Real Lives. It's a game where once you enter you get a virtual life in any part of the globe, in any country on the earth. Depending upon the socio-economic conditions of that country, this virtual person faces challenges like famine, epidemic or floods and earthquakes. And while the player engages himself or herself in facing the unforeseen challenges, he or she also very naturally develops the ability to empathies.

We know, there are some developments that change the game and hence are called as game-changers, but here; the game itself is changing your way to think, to imagine the pain, to identify with the sufferers and also to empathies. I am happy to share that this software engineer is an Indian and his game Real Lives is not only becoming popular but also making a big impact!

Vinay Sahasrabuddhe, President, Indian Council for Cultural Relations (ICCR), India.

Basic Human sensitivity is the mother of ability to empathies. And the origin of sensitivity lies in Gautama Buddha's Karuna or Compassion. COMPASSION OR KARUNA is the essential quality of a Bodhisattva. Karuna is also one of the four Brahma Viharas, or 'sublime states' Compassion indicates the qualities of the heart – love and respect for all living beings. MahaKarauna (Great Compassion) is the last of the 18 virtues of a Buddha. It became a high priority ideal with the rise of Mahayana Ideology from the first century C.E.

As pointed out by an academic in his short essay,* 'Enlightened souls from all religions across the Globe seek to uplift human beings from their suffering. The greatness of Gautama; the Buddha, lies in the fact that he, for the first time in human history, made human suffering as the central point of his philosophical system. In fact, the first precept of his teaching is 'everything is of the nature of suffering' (*sarvam duhkam*, सर्वम् दुक्खम्) which is followed by the doctrine of twelve causes of human suffering known as *dvadasha nidana* (द्वादश निदान) which highlights the fact of suffering, its origin, its cessation, and the path to be followed to overcome it. Wisdom (*prajna*, प्रज्ञा) and Compassion (*karuna*, करूणा) are the two guiding principles in this process of removal of suffering.'

This essay further points out 'Wisdom and compassion are uniquely human qualities. But wisdom without compassion is empty and compassion without wisdom blind. Therefore, Buddha gives equal importance to both. Wisdom i.e. (*prajna*, प्रज्ञा) is defined as an insight in the true nature of reality. Without going into its deep metaphysical meanings in Upanicadic and Buddhist traditions, we may highlight that wisdom lies in carefully examining facts that contradict our beliefs, keeping an open mind rather than being closed-minded, listening to other points of view rather than being bigoted. A person who does this is certainly wise and is certain to arrive at true understanding. The word Compassion is made up of two words, 'co' meaning together and 'passion' meaning a strong feeling. When we see someone in distress and we feel their pain as if it were our own, and strive to eliminate or lessen their pain, then this is compassion. One must understand that all the unique characteristics of human beings, like sharing, readiness to give comfort, sympathy, concern and caring – are all manifestations of nothing but compassion.'

Here, I am also reminded of Mahatma Gandhi, who had elaborately spoken about seven dreaded sins! These sins are Wealth without Work, Pleasure without Conscience, Science without Humanity, Knowledge without Character, Politics without Principles, Commerce without Morality and Worship without Sacrifice! I think, Wisdom without Compassion is the eighth such dreaded sin!

In Western medical ethics, **compassion** serves mainly to define the responsibilities and duties of medical professionals. In contrast, Eastern medical ethics consider developing **compassion** as a prerequisite in becoming a physician and recognize its curing effects. In the traditional medicine of Tibet and **Mongolia**, where Mahayana Buddhism prevails, a physician is seen as an enlightened person who has been thoroughly trained in Buddhist philosophy. In order to become a physician, one should develop **compassion**, which is considered as a path to enlightenment. **Compassion** is not a characteristic but a skill used for therapeutic purposes, which should be mastered through training and meditation, stage by stage.

What is essential for becoming a good physician is perhaps more required to become a good ruler, a good administrator. And this is more expected from a leader who is chosen by the people through a democratic process. Which is why, a value system that recognizes the centrality of compassion is a pre-requisite of a successful democratic regime.

Skepticism about the success of democracy became more pronounced after the third wave of democracy of the post-Second World War era. The presumption, that democracy is the best amongst the available forms of governance and it can be a success in any society has proved to be wrong as in certain parts of the world, democracies have either failed completely or proved to be sham democracies.

While the reasons for the widening acceptability of democracy are not too far to seek, with regards to the reasons behind its apparent failures, changing socio-cultural environment is emerging as the prime reason. The changing texture of international politics, the specter of mindless globalisation and its impact on world population and the threat of terror always round the corner are creating a sense of insecurity leading to narrowing of minds and utter insensitivity towards the less privileged or the marginalized.

Extensive surveys conducted by world-renowned research bodies like Pew Research Center have concluded that while ideas at the core of liberal democracy remain popular among global publics, but commitment to democracy is often found to be weak or suspicious. Multiple factors contribute to this lack of commitment, including perceptions about how well democracy is functioning. And as findings from a new Pew Research Center survey show, views about the performance of democratic systems are decidedly negative in many nations. Across 27 countries polled, a median of 51 per cent is dissatisfied with how democracy is working in their country; just 45 per cent are satisfied. Assessments of how well democracy is working vary considerably across nations.

Renowned political scientist and researcher Pippa Norris presents a brilliant analysis of the diminishing popular trust in the idea of democracy. She says, '...development is most effective where regimes combine the qualities of democratic responsiveness and state effectiveness'. However, one can easily infer that lack of genuine integrity with the concept of democratic responsiveness gives birth to negligence to State effectiveness and again, without a sense of Compassion towards the people, democratic responsiveness always remains superficial and largely, contrived. Compassion is a force that demolishes artificial compartments underscoring the essential elements of equality of human beings and on the basis of this equality, unity of human beings as well.

His Holiness Dalai Lama# in one of his writings has said, "The Buddha saw that life's very purpose is happiness. He also saw that while ignorance binds beings in endless frustration and suffering, wisdom is liberating. Modern democracy is based on the principle that all human beings are essentially equal, that each of us has an equal right to life, liberty, and happiness. Buddhism too recognises that human beings are entitled to dignity, that all members of the human family have an equal and inalienable right to liberty, not just in terms of political freedom, but also at the fundamental level of freedom from fear and want. Irrespective of whether we are rich or poor, educated or uneducated, belonging to one nation or another, to one religion or another, adhering to this ideology or that, each of us is just a human being like everyone else. Not only do we all desire happiness and seek to avoid suffering, but each of us has an equal right to pursue these goals."

Buddhism is essentially a practical doctrine. In recognizing suffering as the fundamental fact of life, Buddhism lays equal stress on individual and community (society). In addressing the fundamental problem of human suffering, it does not insist on a single solution because human beings are not alike in terms of their needs, dispositions and abilities. But as a community its cohesion springs from a unifying sense of brotherhood and sisterhood. Without any apparent centralized authority Buddhism has endured for more than two thousand five hundred years. It has flourished in a diversity of forms, while repeatedly renewing, through study and practice, its roots in the teachings of the Buddha. This kind of pluralistic approach, in which individuals themselves are responsible, is very much in accord with a democratic outlook of the present times.

Many political scientists have pointed out that for sustainable democratic governance, democratic spirit is an essential ingredient of the cultural milieu of the society of the respective country. Right since the ancient period the ideas of Buddha have provided a strong foundation for democracy in general and democratic governance in particular.

True, that if democracy is about accommodation and rejection of monopolistic approach, adherence to the principles of spiritual democracy is a must. Compassion alone can promote spirit of accommodation and resilience and hence Compassion as a value is critical for the success of democracy!

In this context, it is important to note what Dr B R Ambedkar, a political leader and social reformer in modern India who headed the drafting committee for the Constitution of India has said. According to him, the "religion of the Buddha gives freedom of thought and freedom of self-development to all", Ambedkar has also rightly argued that "the rise of Buddhism in India was as significant as the French Revolution."

However, the fact remains that for democracy alone may not help what Buddha wanted to achieve. For enduring peace of mind, Happiness is essential. And it was certainly not just a coincidence that the idea of Gross Human Happiness index originated in Bhutan, a country of the worshippers of Buddha. Happiness, although not entirely or solely but largely also depends upon development with ease of living, at its core. In that sense, democracy that delivers development is the need of the hour. Rulers, motivated by the ideals of Buddha and influenced by his idea of Compassion alone can evolve this fundamental commitment to democracy and not just democracy, but democracy that delivers through development and ease of living.

Democracy that brings development to the deprived is singularly important for a world order that will ensure peaceful coexistence of all. In this context what is further required is evolving a new branch of knowledge or discipline of study, where Confluence of Civilisations will be studied in depth and thereby global society will be sensitized about the need for further strengthening the forces of harmony, dialogue, quest for commonalities and pursuit of common good. Herein lies the concept of mutuality and samanvya, which is reflected very prominently in Hindu-Buddhist traditions.

Before I conclude, I must say that for a world order based on principles of justice and equality, Hindu and Buddhist traditions will have to acquire further strength, become more pronounced and articulate, jointly work for new knowledge creation for generations ahead and in keeping with Buddha's message, of Atta Deepa Bhav, continue to spread light and eliminate darkness from all over the world. If there is any Ulanbaatar Declaration, I believe it is only this!

ANNEXURES

CONCEPT PAPER

SAMVAD-I (2015)

Global Hindu-Buddhist Initiative *on* *Conflict Avoidance and Environment Consciousness*

Organized by

Vivekananda International Foundation, India

In collaboration with

International Buddhist Confederation, India & The Tokyo Foundation, Japan

New Delhi, September 3-4, 2015

I. The Background

A "*Global Hindu–Buddhist Initiative on Conflict Avoidance and Environment Consciousness*" is being organised by the Vivekananda International Foundation in collaboration with the International Buddhist Confederation and Tokyo Foundation.

The conference would be addressing the unprecedented threats and challenges related to peace and environment the world is facing today. Besides traditional, ideological and cultural rivalries, new challenges have emerged in the form of lawless forces backed up by extremely violent ideologies that challenge de-jure states formed on the rule of law. The world order is under threat as never before. In addition, the world is also facing a high degree of ecological degradation due to contemporary life style based on ideas contrary to the environment friendly philosophies that regard nature as sacred and also refer to it as "*mother*".

Overuse and exploitation of nature in the name of development has transformed it into a source used for satisfying our never ending human needs. Driven by myopia of profits, such exploitative nature of humans and their commerce led life styles is threatening the sustainability and survival of our planet. Reckless exploitation of the resources has triggered an environmental breakdown on a planetary scale. Shortage of resources has resulted in mass displacement which further leads to conflicts over control of resources. Majority of the issues are largely related with *"life style"* and cannot be regulated by law or global treaties. A philosophical reorientation is required for which a larger constituency has to be reached by creating more awareness and having dialogues and discussions.

The two main themes for discussion, specially *'conflict avoidance'* bases itself on a democratic framework along with a philosophic tradition which should be friendly and support all forms of lifestyle and governance models, as without a democratic and philosophical foundation having a dialogue or debate on conflict resolution, environment protection and a change in lifestyle based on environmental friendly philosophy wouldn't be possible. Therefore to overcome these emerging challenges an innovative, non-formal and strategic planning has to be done. In the era of rapid globalisation, it is also important for countries now emerging on the global spectrum to take over their responsibilities.

The Global Buddhist Initiative on Conflict Avoidance and Environmental Consciousness is an initiative taken to overcome these challenges. The initiative has a foundation of a strong non-conflicting philosophical paradigm of the two oldest and vibrantly active civilisation forces: Hinduism and Buddhism where non-violence is fundamental to both and, is compatible with the modern democratic values and institutions. The concept on non-violence here extends beyond humanity but also includes *"nature"* as a part of human life. Hinduism and Buddhism are centered on non-violence and compassion towards not only humans, but also animals and plants- labeling them as ecologically compatible philosophies. In context with environmental consciousness the foundation of these two philosophies as well as those of Shinto and Confucianism is based on *"Ethical Behavior"*. A short sutta in the Anguttara Nikaya (4:115), provides a discerning piece of counsel on treatment of the environment, distinguishing between actions that are pleasant in the short run but harmful in the long term, and actions that are disagreeable in the short run but conducive to long term benefit. A detailed narrative of the background to this initiative thus will bring home its need and the rationale.

II. World Needs a Paradigm Shift from Conflict Resolution to Conflict Avoidance

The prognosis, once dismissed, that the traditional religious and ideological rivalries and clashes along cultures would return, seems to be very much on the horizon. The world today is on a totally different tangent emanating from galloping religious and ideological conflicts escalating and thus leading to terrorism and massive violent destruction. Terrorists, who were once described as *"non-state actors"* are now controlling large parts of territories and also challenging the power and authority of de jure states that are responsible for the so called *"world order"*. Massive violence has been unleashed against innocent people who differ even a shade in faith or thoughts from the extremists. All these extremely violent and destructive activities have pressurised the intellectuals, the leaders and the strategic thinkers to develop an alternative ways to tackle these situations.

Despite the danger signals being quite evident since a couple of decades, no significant collective or strategic efforts were made to prepare and shape the world opinion to avoid present conflicts. This is solely because the world, since world war II has moved the paradigm of *"conflict resolution"* instead of *"conflict avoidance"*. This paradigm has severe limitations and therefore, there is a need to modify the future paradigm as ***"conflict avoidance"***.

III. Philosophical Dialogues for Conflict Avoidance

> *"No peace among the nations, without peace among the religions. No peace among the religions, without dialogue between the religions" – HANS KUNG*

The intellectuals of today have excluded the idea of philosophy and are caught up in the cobweb of rigid ideologies which exclude *"the other"* view along with dialogue which leads to conflicts. The current approach towards conflict resolution is also largely based on western and simplified perspectives of conflict between faiths and civilisations. Therefore, it is in this context that the world is increasingly noticing the benign nature of Buddhism vis-a-vis western ethics. Therefore, it is important to recognise the importance of historical Asian traditions and values to make them more relevant for the future of world peace and harmony, especially the culture of understanding and acceptance of the alternative view beyond that of mercy and tolerance. Unfortunately, learning from traditions has been lost in Asian discourse, which now requires close attention due to alarming global threats. The Hindu- Buddhist values can be used as a tool to shift the paradigm to *"conflict avoidance"* and the path of *"ideology"* to *"philosophy"*. Clearly, both understanding as well as mapping of Asia with its dynamic cross-cultural pollination needs new focus to determine how we could apply such values of *"acceptance of the other view"* as integral to diversity across national boundaries, and not merely within them. Therefore, identification of the key elements of the Asian civilisations is important in order to find an alternative democratic vision and also consolidate cooperation among nations so that people collectively participate and prosper.

IV. Non-Conflicting Cultures and Fusion of Democratic Forces

It's quite evident that high risk situations cannot be handled by the existing geopolitical arrangements and institutions therefore besides the new paradigm of conflict avoidance; new strategies are required to de-escalate terrorism, disorder and extremism. Another important cause of extremism and violence, besides the centrifugal power of violent ideologies, is the absences of *"democratic governance"* in many parts of the world along with a lack of space in the global disclosure for the non-conflicting civilisations which have an accommodative anti-dote for conflict prone ideologies. There is thus a need for a democratic approach, which not only accommodates but also harmonises diversities. The world today requires medium and long term efforts from the non-conflicting faiths and cultures to combine with democratic forces, and to confront the rising tide of violence threatening the world order. It shall also help us build a non-formal intellectual and geopolitical architecture to appeal, influence, persuade and moderate the forces of violence. In order to acquire this, intense studies through established and new think tanks about the sources and impulses of violence to effectively counter them is required. For this purpose, non-formal interaction and strategic co-operation among all non-conflicting and democratic societies and nations would be needed unravel the causes of conflict and preventing from escalating.

V. Asian Thoughts: Universal Responsibility and Environmental Consciousness

The practice of *"ethical values"*, which basically refers to personal restraint in consumption and *"environmental consciousness"* are deeply rooted in the ancient Asian philosophical traditions especially in the virtues of Hinduism and Buddhism. It is remarkable how effectively Hinduism and Buddhism in their extremely flexible and responsive stances in the history have been able to nurture and preserve the culture of not just tolerance, but also acceptance of all faiths and cultures along with inculcating democratic and ethical values.

The diversity of Asian value systems particularly the role of Buddhism, as a form of thought and the traditions of Indian thinking reflected and incorporated in Hinduism, have had a profound impact on the rest of Asia. Being inherently inclusive and therefore naturally tolerant of diversity of cultural conventions, both have been able to overcome the ready arguments of Asian divisibility at various turns of history. Therefore, by placing themselves in the interstices of local cultures and polities, Buddhism and Hinduism effectively interweaved myriad societies and built a culture of ethical values among social and political elites in Asia.

VI. Environmental Challenges and Role of Religions

Humankind is on a collision with the biological limits of the earth and now *"conversation"* has become a moral issue of beauty, ethics and spiritual values. Buddhism along with other faiths such as Confucianism, Taoism and Shintoism has undertaken a much greater responsibly for protecting the environment upon which the survival of all depends. Over exploitation of natural resources, deforestation, melting of glaciers, ever increasing exploration for hydrocarbons and pollution in general etc have become the causes of climate change and is leading the world towards catastrophe.

Alas these pitfalls will not stop mankind from its unbridled indulgence. On the contrary we are witnessing flash points across the globe due to the race, to control and harness these resources among nations and communities. Horrendous crimes against both humanity and nature are being committed with alarming impunity.

Therefore, Hinduism and Buddhism with their well defined treaties on respect for Mother Nature can create a huge impact and lead towards a "*sustainable world.*" Buddha's 2600 year old message about kindness, personal responsibility, and the path to happiness holds the key to a new way of relating to each other and to our environment. Therefore, there is an urgent need for a strategic action to mitigate the merging environmental woes which lead to conflict at various levels. The conference shall thus examine the environmental changes we are facing at present and how Buddhism and Hinduism can/should respond to them.

VI. The Initiative

We are of the view that adaptation of a non-conflicting paradigm which is inclusive of philosophic streams such as Buddhism and Hinduism whose adherents account for more than one-fifth of the world's population; cognates cultures such as Indian and Japanese which can effectively undertake the initiative in promoting democratic values, religious understandings and conflict avoidance in the larger interest for the world.

We believe that Asia can certainly offer a new model and vision for a world order based on its democratic tradition that espouses the spirit of human cooperation, ethical behaviour, universal responsibility and prosperity of all nations.

It is with this aspiration and conviction that the Vivekananda International Foundation (VIF), New Delhi proposes to hold a Conference in collaboration with Tokyo Foundation and International Buddhist Confederation (IBC) on *"Global Hindu-Buddhist Initiative on Conflict Avoidance and Environment Consciousness"* to be held in India on September 3-4, 2015.

VII. The Objectives

The identified objectives for the proposed conferences are:

- To emphasise and espouse that democratic and non-conflicting philosophies, which are fundamental to conflict avoidance, and inherent to Asian values found in Hinduism, Buddhism and other indigenous religions and philosophies;
- To review historical sources and literature on the practice of democracy, analyze and enhance the contributions of Asian spiritual and political thoughts to the foundation of democracy in Asia, as well as, reassess their value as the basis of democracy in contemporary Asia;
- To seek plan of actions for creating a conducive and compelling eco-system with the final objective of avoiding conflicts inherent in exclusive ideologies, and emphasising the importance of dialogue and understanding;
- To launch a transparent dialogue among non-conflicting philosophic traditions in Asia and discuss the prospects of evolving long-term perspective for promoting democratic values and institutions critical to future development;
- To institute a sustainable model of open and frank dialogue with and within conflict-prone ideologies;
- To engage with ideological groups and persuade re-interpretation of

rigid ideological premises to make them moderate, inclusive and accommodative of other views;

- To conduct studies and global level dialogues and debates to find and suggest ways and institutional means by which the conflict-prone elements in the exclusive ideologies could be moderated or eliminated for the good of their adherents and for the good of world peace and harmony;
- To bring environment consciousness in global discourse and promote significant changes to the way our present economic system is structured that is in conflict with nature and unsustainable
- To establish a global network of leaders in a wide range of social, political, environmental and intellectual arena committed to the promotion of democratic values, conflict avoidance, environmental consciousness, universal responsibility and ethical behaviours rooted in Asia;
- To encourage regular dialogue in order to promote constructive debate on issues critical for promoting Asian values of peaceful coexistence between humanity, and also with nature, in the context of establishing genuine global peace and secure earth.

VIII. The Outcomes

- Institution of a mechanism to work for transparent philosophic discussions on conflict avoidance and environment protection at the global level.
- Co-opting Global Institutions to take up the agenda of the Initiative and carry on dialogue and debate on the themes.
- Taking the themes to leading thought institutions, academia of the world.

IX. Sessions & Talks

The format of the two day conference will be thematic and the topics beings discussed on the respective days are listed below:

- Conflict Avoidance
- Environment Protection

Besides inauguration and valedictory there will be full two technical sessions namely pre and post lunch sessions. However, themes for the technical session will remain same as mentioned above. There will be one key note speaker per session and ten speakers per theme.

Discussion papers will be circulated on both themes with adequate background papers well in time for the participants to understand the issues.

It is aimed to comprehensively seek to address myriad challenges in Asia i.e. spread of conflict, transnational terror networks and sectarian violence, climate change, environmental degradation and conservation issues etc from an Asian perspective and also suggest creative solutions and sustainable social, economic and political framework for management of conflict and fostering cooperation and promote environmental consciousness and interdependent universal responsibility.

SAMVAD-II (2017)

Dialogue for Peace, Harmony and Security

A Global Initiative for Conflict Avoidance and Environment Consciousness

Organisers

Vivekananda International Foundation (VIF), India and Sitagu International Buddhist Academy (SIBA), Myanmar

In association with

Myanmar Institute of Strategic and International Studies (MISIS), Myanmar & The Japan Foundation

A conference titled "**Samvad**" held on 3-4 September 2015 in New Delhi was a profound, path breaking and landmark event which was perceived as having the potential to change the global discourse on the themes of "Conflict Avoidance" and "Environmental Consciousness".

Organised by Vivekananda International Foundation, Delhi and The Tokyo Foundation, Tokyo, in association with the International Buddhist Confederation [IBC], it was the joint enterprise of two of the oldest, living, tolerant, non-conflicting civilisations and philosophies.

Hindu and Buddhist philosophies accept other thought and belief systems as valid for their respective followers which makes them doctrinally tolerant. These two philosophies which have common origin and retained their mutual and symbiotic relations, also believe, within and outside, in dialogue as the normal way to create and sustain human consciousness and avoid conflicts. Doctrinally tolerant and with propensity for dialogue both philosophies inhere their potential for conflict avoidance. Again both these civilisations regard nature as sacred, which makes them exceptionally environment conscious. Therefore, their nature-friendly tenets have the potential to preserve the environment and ecology.

With their conflict-avoiding propensities and environment-compatible nature, these two civilisations have the philosophic potential to build a global conflict-avoidance architecture and also ingrain and implant environment consciousness in people by recalling their spiritual worldview that the divine is immanent as much in nature as in humans.

The Conference, which was a joint endeavour of these two civilisations was conceived as an ambitious, yet not an unachievable, goal to shift the paradigm of global discourse on the two critical issues – of *conflicts* from **Conflict Resolution to Conflict Avoidance** and of *Environment* from **Environmental Regulations** to **Environmental Consciousness.** In a world which seems to be running short of ideas other than government action to defend and preserve environment, the conference seeks to open people-participatory paradigm on both conflict avoidance and environmental consciousness.

Appropriately titled "Samvad", a derivative of the Sanskrit word *"Samvadam"* [meaning "Dialogue"], the speakers at the conference urged open and truthful global dialogue on conflicts and the environment.

The heart of the Conference was captured in the Key Note Paper presented at the meeting, which informed the discussions during the two days of the conference. The Key Note Paper was centred on seeking three fundamental changes or paradigm shifts:

- One, from curative conflict resolution to preventive conflict avoidance.
- Two, from state environmental regulations to mass ecological consciousness.
- Three, from the dialogue-evasive ideology to dialogue-friendly philosophy.

The conference themes are not mutually exclusive. They are interrelated through the underlying value of dialogue, which the third limb emphasises. The Key Note Paper could be the basis for all future conferences involving conflict avoidance and environmental consciousness.

All religions primarily promote peace and harmony, yet conflict resolution ideas and structures are becoming weak and inadequate, needing an alternative approach. The conflict avoidance paradigm promoted in the Delhi meet rests on the view that Hans Kungs, a religious theologian of the Roman Catholic Church, formulated, which postulated *that peace among nations is not possible without peace among religions, peace among religions is not possible without dialogue among religions and dialogue among religions is impossible without investigating the fundamentals of different religions.* Thus, open and transparent philosophic dialogue, which is inherent in Asiatic traditions, forms the core of the conflict avoidance paradigm suggested by Hans Kungs.

Again, the current paradigm of resolving conflict between humans and development on the one side and the environment on the other is government regulation which does not treat the cause of the environmental degradation rooted in anthropocentric belief, thought and development systems which again have as their source from the theological systems which deny sacredness to nature and therefore refuse to accept reverence for nature. The alternative paradigm of human reverence for sacred nature for resolving the conflict between humans and the environment is deeper than even deep environmental consciousness, which is now being discussed in intellectual circles in the West. The alternative paradigm of environmental consciousness based on these civilisation's reverence for the sacredness of nature is rooted in the cultural and religious principles of environmentally conscious belief systems, which has the potential to transform the present ruling paradigm of the anthropocentric development model into an eco-centric one.

Environmental issues also call for dialogue among religions and belief systems to promote the consciousness that nature is sacred and as sacred as humans. All dialogues on the fundamentals of any ideology – including religions – will help transform dialogue evasive ideologies into dialogue-promoting philosophies that govern the paradigm of conflict avoidance.

The Delhi Samvad Conference was thus an endeavour to transform the meeting into a new movement – a global intellectual and civilisational movement to create deep awareness about, spread, and advocate the three themes in global discourse. This conference was intended as the beginning of the process, with a series of conferences first in Asian nations to carry and deepen the agenda and later in other places.

The Prime Minister of India inaugurated the Delhi conference in the august presence of world leaders, and most eminent spiritual masters of Buddhist, Hindu and other faiths Venerable Buddhist monks and nuns from India, Japan, Sri Lanka, Bhutan, Cambodia, Mongolia, Myanmar, Thailand, Bangladesh, Nepal, Hong Kong, Singapore, and Vietnam and eminent Buddhist scholars from Australia, UK, USA, Switzerland, Belgium, Germany and Russia participated in the two-day conference. The Hindu delegates who participated were largely from India and Nepal. The Prime Minister also joined the delegates at the Sacred Mahabodhi temple in the Holy City of Bodhgaya on September 5, 2015, where the Bodhgaya Declaration was adopted.

Our partners, The Tokyo Foundation & Japan Foundation, followed the initiative by hosting a symposium on 'Shared Values and Democracy in Asia' in Tokyo on 19 January 2016. The Prime Minister of Japan Mr. Shinzo Abe delivered the key note speech.

The Conference at Yangon on August 5-6, 2017, is proposed to follow up on the Samvad Initiative, expounding, articulating, and deepening the philosophic understanding on the two issues of critical importance to the world: shifting the paradigm from conflict resolution to conflict avoidance and environmental regulation to environmental consciousness.

There have been positive developments subsequent to the Delhi meet. For the first time, the environmental philosophic perspectives of these two civilisations were expressed at the Paris Climate Summit in November 2015. The religious leaders belonging to the two oldest philosophies of the world presented separately the perspectives of their philosophies as to how to handle the climate challenge. The two presentations had many common points as a result of the Delhi meeting.

The environmental theme of the Delhi meeting was taken to the Paris Climate Meet by the Hon'ble Prime Minister of India in two ways: one, he penned a book that contained the philosophic dimensions of the meet on environmental consciousness; two, he and the French President released a musical album produced by the VIF with the help of Grammy Award winner Ricky Kej [in which 300 artistes from across the world participated] which contained the civilisational hymns from environment-compatible religious literature which formed the basis of the Samvad meet in Delhi.

The UN General Assembly has now passed a resolution on 'Culture and Sustainable Development'. The UN resolution in substance endorses the environmental theme of the HBC regarding environmental consciousness and the Samvad concept paper that linked culture to sustainable development. This shows that the world is prepared to explore the civilisational and philosophical roots to seek solutions to the crises endangering the world's very existence. It is suggested that the Key Note Paper of the Delhi meeting and UN resolution could be the foundation for the deliberations at the Yangon leg of the meeting.

SAMVAD-III (2019)

Global Hindu–Buddhist Initiative for Conflict Avoidance and Environment Consciousness

Dialogue for Peaceful Co-existence, Inter-religious Understanding and Interdependent Sustainability

Organizers

Vivekananda International Foundation (VIF), India and Gandan Tegchenling Monastery and Institute of Strategic Studies of the National Security Council of Mongolia

In association with

Asian Buddhist Conference for Peace (ABCP), International Buddhist Confederation (IBC) & The Japan Foundation

Proposed venue: Gandan Tegchenling Monastery, Ulaanbaatar, Mongolia

6-7 September 2019

Background

SAMVAD was born out of a dialogue between the Indian Prime Minister Narendra Modi and Japanese Prime Minister Shinzo Abe to apply the spiritual teachings of Hinduism and Buddhism to address modern-day issues threatening human civilisation. It was felt that spiritual masters and experts should engage in a frank, honest and all-encompassing dialogue to generate an alternative narrative and vision based on the spirit of understanding, accommodation, ethical behaviour, universal responsibility in order to shift the global discourse on the two critical issues facing humankind e.g. **Conflict Avoidance and Environmental Degradation.** Hindu, Buddhist and most of the cultures rooted in Asian and Indic philosophies have tolerant civilizational approach. They accept other thoughts and belief systems as valid for their respective followers. They regard dialogue even on what are regarded as unalterable fundamentals as the normal and the best way to avoid conflicts. Further, the Asian and Indic civilizations regard nature as sacred. They recognise the interdependence between nature and all species including humankind and they are ecocentric and not anthropocentric. They stress on the need for people-participatory approach by going back to fundamentals of their spiritual discourse on environment consciousness. They emphasise the need for a shift from exploitation of nature to respect and harmony with nature.

The Buddhist concept of **interdependent origination** applies to everything in the world and Hindu philosophical perspective of Isavasyam Idam Sarvam [meaning everything down to the tiniest atom is manifestation of the Divine] that revers nature and Mother Earth enshrine authentic environmental consciousness. This needs to be inculcated by recognising the deep interdependence between humans, plants, and animals. Far more than environmental regulation, environmental consciousness is critical to the future of our planet as the effects of climate change, extinction of species and natural imbalance, the natural disasters and ecological problems do not choose people of one religion or one nation but impacts entire planet.

Appropriately titled "Samvad", with origins in the Sanskrit word *"Samvadam"* [meaning "Dialogue"], the initiative seeks to build a grassroots movement based on open and truthful global dialogue seeking three paradigm-shifts:

- One, from curative conflict resolution to preventive conflict avoidance.
- Two, from state environmental regulations to mass ecological consciousness.
- Three, from the dialogue-evasive ideology to dialogue-friendly philosophy.

Samvad initiative is aimed to create a conducive and compelling eco-system with the objective of emphasizing the importance of dialogue and understanding for avoiding conflicts and bring environment consciousness in global discourse and restructuring of present economic system that is inherently unsustainable and in conflict with nature. As the world faces the grim consequences of environmental degradation inflicted through wanton destruction of nature and species for human consumption and greed that produced wastefulness and uncompassionate society it is very critical to inculcate environmental consciousness amongst current and future generation for the survival of the world and the only planet, we live in.

Samvad, thus calls for instituting sustainable institutional model for frank and open dialogues between non-conflicting philosophies, ideologies and evolving a long-term perspective for promoting institutions to carry forward ideas generated though these dialogues for lasting peace, harmony and security. It endeavours for establishing a global network of leaders in a wide range of social, political, environmental and intellectual arena committed to the promotion of democratic values, conflict avoidance, environmental consciousness, universal responsibility and ethical behaviour.

The Initiative: Driven by the above thought, a landmark and path breaking conference titled "**Samvad: A Global Hindu–Buddhist Initiative for Conflict Avoidance & Environment Consciousness**" was organized on 3-4 September 2015 in New Delhi jointly by Vivekananda International Foundation, Delhi and The Tokyo Foundation, Tokyo, along with International Buddhist Confederation [IBC]. It was inaugurated by Prime Minister of India in New Delhi in the august company of former President of Sri Lanka Mrs Chandrika Kumaratunga, the ministers from Japan, Mongolia, Nepal and Bhutan. The Japanese Prime Minister also delivered a video message on the occasion. The then External Affairs Minister of India, Mrs. Sushma Swaraj delivered the Valedictory Address. On the Closing Day, on 5th September 2015, the Prime Minister Modi led the participants and dignitaries in prayers and meditation under the Holy Bodhi Tree at the Mahabodhi Temple in Bodhgaya on the very sacred grounds of Enlightened Awakening of Buddha. A **Bodhgaya Declaration** was also adopted.

A series of Conferences and Symposiums followed, including two in Tokyo in 2016 and 2018 on the theme 'Shared Values & Democracies in Asia' and Samvad-II in Yangon, Myanmar. The Japanese Prime Minister delivered the special addresses on both the occasions and Prime Minister of India addressed the audience via video messages.

The Yangon, Myanmar, edition of Samvad was another successful step forward in carrying the initiative to a region experiencing conflict and an endeavour to build a platform for frank and open dialogue among interfaith religious leadership on the roots of conflict. The extensive deliberations by religious and political leaders, leading scholars and environmental experts firmly established the need for a paradigm shift from ideological and consummative approach towards a philosophical and accommodative approach to address global challenges. It called for creating a more tolerant, liberal and accommodative world based on mutual respect and acceptability of diversity of views and living in harmony with nature rather than seeing it as a resource to exploit.

Prime Minister Shri Narendra Modi in his video speech referred to critical questions about global challenges the world is facing today like conflicts and climate change. He stressed that "it is only through deep and prolonged dialogue – *Samvad* – that we may discover hidden synergies, resolving contradictions and only way to cut though deep rooted religious stereotypes, prejudices that divide communities across the world and sow seeds of conflicts". He referred to Hindu-Buddhist philosophical approach of living in harmony with nature and the need for revering nature and not just see it as a resource to exploit. Japanese Prime Minister Shinzo Abe in his video message invoked Buddhist principles of tolerance and compassion that encompasses coexistence of all lives. He warned that the spirit of tolerance is facing challenges today and terrorism and violent extremism are threatening to deny the existence of 'others' and trying to paint our world in a single colour". He stressed that in Asia "we must let flowers of all different colours bloom in harmony." Noble laureate and State Counsellor of Myanmar, Daw Aung San Suu Kyi, in her speech (which was read out by her NSA) termed Conflict Avoidance as a building block for establishing "community peace", "regional peace" and "global peace". Towards this she called on religious leaders to spread the intrinsic noble teachings, virtues of tolerance and non-violence as embedded in every world religion to their followers and at the grassroots levels and get them to practice these teachings in true essence.

A **Round Table Summit of Spiritual Masters** was introduced for the first time in Yangon edition of Samvad. This was attended by most eminent spiritual leaders of Buddhism, Hinduism, Islam, Christianity, Sikhism and Jainism. Speakers at both the Round Table and the Academic session: *Evolving A Non-Conflicting Philosophical Paradigm for Conflict Avoidance, Peace & Harmony* stressed on the principle of freedom of practicing their own religion without any interference from others. All agreed that trying to force beliefs and ideologies on others has been a major reason for strife and destruction of many a civilisation throughout history and continues to be so. Importance of an honest and open dialogue and the capacity to listen to the alternate viewpoints through platforms such as Samvad offers an opportunity to analyse the threats and challenges to world peace and suggesting sustainable approaches such as the need for adopting non-conflicting ideologies. Any dialogue would certainly be counterproductive if anyone alleged that other religions are false or label the adherents of other religions as sinners, lesser or non-believers. It was also pointed out that there will always be people trying to hijack religion to suit their vested interests and hidden agendas. These elements would twist and turn the truths and translate them in line with their sinister plans and they should not be looked upon as role models for any religion. Deliberations at the Round Table Summit indicated the openness and deep desire among religious leaders for a dialogue beyond the cliché and tokenism that most interfaith and peace initiatives have been reduced to. Despite different perspectives all converged on finding a common platform and common ground for sustainable peace and secure Mother Earth.

The deliberations focussed on evolving a consensus on Action Plan and create institutional means to take the Samvad initiative to grassroots and sustainable eco system for dialogue among non-conflicting philosophical traditions and with conflict prone ideologies. Based on these the **Yangon Declaration** was unanimously adopted.

The Way Forward

The Samvad initiative so far have indicated an overwhelming consensus to find an alternate narrative to issues and crises confronting human civilization and the urgent need to open *"people-participatory paradigm"* on Conflict Avoidance and Environmental Consciousness at both *"macro and micro level"* in addition to actions by governments, multilateral and global bodies. It has given us the lead to pursue that path by

- Making SAMVAD process to grow on a more formalised basis; and
- that the non-conflicting philosophies may be able to lead the world in promoting a sustainable model of conflict avoidance based on respect for all religions, philosophies, coexistence and understanding and Environment Consciousness for humans and nature living in interdependent harmony.

The Samvad III at Ulaanbaatar, Mongolia, is another step in the direction to shift the paradigm of global discourse and build a global architecture on the two critical issues – of Conflicts from **Conflict Resolution to Conflict Avoidance** and of *Environment* from **Environmental Regulations** to **Environmental Consciousness.** In a world which seems to be running short of ideas other than government action to defend and preserve environment, the conference will seek to carry forward the initiative for people-participatory paradigm on both conflict avoidance and environmental consciousness.

(Bodhgaya Declaration & Yangon Declaration will be added with the concept note)

DECLARATION

The Bodh Gaya Declaration 2015

This Bodh Gaya declaration of Buddhist spiritual and temporal leaders, scholars, philosophers and thinkers is made in Bodh Gaya at the conclusion of day-long devotional and spiritual accomplishments.

It is hereby declared that:

1. Bodh Gaya, where Siddhartha became Buddha, is the seat of enlightenment for the world of Buddhism and Buddhist civilization that have inspired all religions of the world.
2. In this age of increasing conflicts where in the last 15 years religious conflicts have trebled and killings in the name of religion have gone up by two-thirds, the spiritual gift of Buddha is the only hope for the world to overcome the intra-religious and inter-religious strife and massacre.
3. The Hindu-Buddhist civilizations have a special responsibility to work for conflict avoidance and environment consciousness by expounding the philosophical principles common to Hinduism and Buddhism to save the world from fratricidal conflicts.
4. The Hindu-Buddhist civilizations, that celebrate diversity and are non-conflicting with other religions, will have to work together for a paradigm shift from the present conflict resolution model powered by geo-politics to conflict avoidance model inspired by civilization.
5. This will call for in-depth spiritual orientation to present an alternative world-view as a new paradigm for understanding, appreciating and celebrating diversity based on the ancient idea of Dhamma as in Pali and Dharma as in Sanskrit.
6. There is no place more appropriate and elevating than Bodh Gaya for inspiring and institutionalizing such noble work.
7. Bodh Gaya has the credentials to emerge, and must emerge, as the global symbol and vehicle for enlightenment, peace and hope for civilizational, spiritual and cultural harmony.

8. A Buddhist spiritual and civilizational institution that will bring together and make the entire Buddhist world participate in this momentous task will be built in Bodh Gaya in the coming three years.
9. Hindu civilizational and spiritual institutions will be invited to work with this new Buddhist institution to share the responsibility for global peace and harmony.
10. Buddhist spiritual leaders will approach governments of all Buddhist nations to support this monumental and noble task of developing Bodh Gaya as an International Centre of Buddhism for the enlightenment of all humankind.
11. We call for support from the Government of India for the development of infrastructure and other public utilities in the area.
12. A team of experts will be constituted to begin the noble work and the responsibility for this purpose shall be given to a committee.

The Yangon Declaration 2017

We unanimously agree and declare on this 6th Day of the Month of August 2017 that:

1. All the people of the world have to cooperate and endeavour together, without any fear, in order to obtain a harmonious social life with full security assurances.
2. We denounce all kinds of hate speech, false propaganda, conflict and war under the pretext of religion and strongly condemn those who provide support for any such activities.
3. We, leaders of all religions of the world, resolve to be builders of a harmonious human society by religious teachings and involve ourselves in consolidating peace and security in the world.
4. We, members of different faiths, need to build mutual understanding, respect and trust among ourselves in order to obtain a peaceful, secure and prosperous human society.
5. We resolve to exercise restraint and, refrain from interfering in matters of other religions and to cooperate in building bridges for world peace.
6. It is our inherent duty to conserve the environment before it is too late for the survival of humankind.
7. All religious leaders from India present at this Samvad II have unanimously decided to meet once every four months (and as and when required), starting 4 December 2017, to build bridges and harmony.
8. We shall collectively initiate programmes to enhance environmental consciousness and undertake awareness/ protection projects.
9. To strengthen understanding and trust, we shall organise an interfaith camp for meditation.
10. All the spiritual paths and religious traditions are equally valid.

The Ulaanbaatar Declaration 2019

Two Round Tables were organised as part of the Samvad Global Hindu-Buddhist Initiative for Conflict Avoidance, Inter-Religious Understanding, and Interdependent Sustainability, which was held in Ulaanbaatar, Mongolia, on September 6 and 7, 2019. One was the Religious Round Table on Conflict Avoidance and Inter-Religious Understanding, and the other was the Round Table on Environmental Consciousness and Interdependent Sustainability.

The Religious Round Table (RRT) expresses its deep concern over the propensity and potential for conflicts and also the declining environment both of which pose increasing challenges to global peace and prosperity.

The RRT of religious leaders and scholars is that leaders of different faiths owe a responsibility to promote conflict avoidance and environmental consciousness.

During the discussions, the tendency among some faiths to divide the people as faithful and non-believers with an attendant 'divine' mandate to convert 'non-believers' into 'believers' was pointed out as one of the principal causes of conflicts. The RRT felt that unless this is checked, it will tend to promote the propensity among powerful sections of them to push their 'divine' agenda against such 'believers' either trying to buy 'non-believers' or exterminate them through extremism and terror. This obviously leads to endless conflicts and violence in the world.

Her Excellency Daw Aung San Suu Kyi, the State Counsellor of The Republic of the Union of Myanmar, has sent a message to the Ulaanbaatar Initiative. The RRT considers the following parts of her message relevant in the context of its discussions and also the current challenges:

> *[S]ome of the responsible religionists do not take interest in imparting knowledge of the genuine knowledge of the genuine teachings shown by their respective religions. Moreover, some even lead their followers to the wrong way by means of instructing then bogus and insincere doctrines under the name of religion.*

The RRT discussed the different terminologies employed by different religions to distinguish between their faithful's and others which leads to how the faith and the faithfuls should perceive them and treat them. The RRT feels that the religious leaders and scholars should review the use of those terms so as to remove the apprehensions in the minds of the other faiths and their followers about the intent of the terms employed.

The RRT also is of the view that dialogue among religions is inevitable for conflict avoidance. The RRT is inclined to adopt that formula of the Catholic Theologian Hans Kung for dialogue. Hans Kung said that:

> *"Unless their peace between religions there can be no peace between nations.*
>
> *Two, there cannot be peace between religions unless there is dialogue among religions.*
>
> *And, three, there cannot be meaningful dialogue among religions unless the foundations of each religion are researched."*

The Hans Kung principles were originally to be found in the Hindu Buddhist dialogue discipline of *Tarka Shastra* and *Purva Paksha* which both of them employed to debate their differences. One of the reasons for the lack of violence among religions in the Hindu Buddhist civilisations has been the practice of dialogue.

The RRT feels that unless the differences among religions are discussed and debated in dialogues like *Samvad*, the differences will be settled in streets.

The RRT is of the view that in the contemporary world no religion can claim exclusivity and assert that its fundamentals cannot be questioned by other faiths, particularly if such fundamentals affect the other faiths and their adherents.

The RRT therefore commends that all religions need to foster the discipline of dialogue within and develop internal tolerance without which there cannot be external tolerance.

The RRT appeals to all religious leaders that we need to build a tolerant world first and then move towards a world where each religion accepts that other religions are also capable of leading human beings to good conduct and salvation.

The RRT expresses the hope that the different religions will adopt initiatives like *Samvad* and RRT to carry forward the consensus reached in Ulaanbaatar.

The RT of Environmental Consciousness and Interdependent Sustainability is of the view that in the name of 'development' Mother Nature continues to be abused. As a result, large parts of the globe are regularly under drought or floods. Our rivers and lakes are more polluted than ever before. Even the survival of marine life in fathomless oceans is threatened by senseless dumping of waste by humans.

The reckless exploitation of natural resources over centuries has brought the Mother Earth to a dangerous pass. Can humanity be safe, if the survival of the planet itself is in danger? The RT feels that religions should propagate the environment friendly texts in their religions and should do away and drop the aspects of the text which are environmentally not compatible.

The RT is of the view that role of traditional wisdom and faiths in pursuing sustainable development has not been fully appreciated so far. This conference stresses the need to secure indigenous faiths and practices which invariably are eco-friendly.

The RT is convinced that the local practices and traditions are usually the result of centuries of interaction and interplay between humans and nature. Any alien efforts in the name of 'civilising' the locals or 'development' disrupts this beautiful relationship and leads to disaster.

The RT urges that the religions work to rein in human greed, respect Mother Nature and recognise and appreciate the role of traditional societies in maintaining the ecological balance.

REPORTS

Global Conclave on 'Hindu-Buddhist Initiative on Conflict Avoidance and Environment Consciousness' (New Delhi/Bodh Gaya 2015)

The Vivekananda International Foundation (VIF) jointly organised a three-day global conclave, 'Samvad: Hindu-Buddhist Initiative on Conflict Avoidance and Environment Consciousness', in collaboration with the International Buddhist Federation and The Tokyo Foundation, from 3 to 5 September 2015. Proceedings of the conclave were conducted during the first two days at VIF in New Delhi, while the venue was shifted to Bodh Gaya in Bihar on the third day. The conclave was inspired by Prime Minister Narendra Modi's vision of highlighting India's civilisational links with the world. The Prime Minister inaugurated the conclave in Delhi and went to Bodh Gaya with the delegates to offer a special prayer for global peace and harmony under the Bodhi Tree at the Mahabodhi temple, Buddhism's holiest shrine. A pre-recorded message from Japan's Prime Minister Shinzo Abe was also played during the inaugural session of the conference.

While Mr. Shinzo Abe, in his recorded message, said Japan owed its 'rule of law' to Buddhism, Prime Minister Narendra Modi emphasised that teachings of Hinduism and Buddhism can provide answers to many of the problems the world faces, especially the ones related to conflicts and environmental degradation. Hon'ble Modi's resounding speech underlined the emerging dangers to the world and the environment. He stressed that the quintessence of resolving conflicts lies in dialogue. Expressing his deep anguish over the rising level of conflicts across societies, the Prime Minister emphasised that the theme of dialogue on conflicts needs to shift from an ideological approach to a philosophical one. It was evident from his speech that the world needs a fresh approach to deal with the twin threats of rising conflicts and environmental degradation.

Delegates from over 15 countries, including Sri Lanka, Nepal, Bhutan, Myanmar, Thailand, Vietnam, Cambodia, Japan, Taiwan, and a few European countries, participated in the conference. Union Minister of State for Home Affairs, Mr Kiren Rijiju and Union Minister of State (Independent Charge) for Culture, Tourism and MoS for Ministry of Civil Aviation, Mr Mahesh Sharma, were among other distinguished invitees to the conference.

The conclave on the first day focused on the issue of conflict avoidance. From the discussions held amongst the scholars, it came out loud and clear that the teachings of Gautama Buddha, Swami Vivekananda and other spiritual leaders of Hinduism and Buddhism, especially on inter-religious tolerance and peaceful co-existence, are more relevant today than ever before. Speaker after speaker agreed that this conclave offered a great opportunity to analyse threats and challenges to the maintenance of world peace and tranquillity. There was total consensus that there was a need to break away from ideological shackles and start a philosophical debate to develop a global understanding as a means of avoiding conflicts.

Sri Lanka's former President, Mrs Chandrika Kumartunga, Japan's State Minister for Foreign Affairs; Mr Minoru Kiuchi, Founder of the Art of Living Foundation; Sri Sri Ravi Shankar, Secretary General of the International Buddhist Confederation Ven. Lama Lobzang, Ven. Thich Nhat Tu from Vietnam, Founder of Dharmashree Gita Parivar & Mahirshi Ved Vyas Pratishthan Swami Govind Dev Giri and Shri Swaminathan Gurumurthy, among others, discussed ways and means of avoiding conflicts in a world-torn apart by religious fanaticism and ideological bigotry.

The second day witnessed a spirited and composite dialogue among the participants on environmental consciousness being the prime paradigm of socio-cultural cooperation and creative global action. The philosophical underpinnings of Buddhist dharma were touched upon in reference to the protection of natural heritage and the pursuit of sustainable growth. Environmental protection could be possible only with such awareness based on our ancient beliefs with respect to Mother Earth.

With Param Pujya Swami Paramatmananda, Secretary General & Coordinator of Hindu Dharma Acharya Sabha, India, and Ven. Telo Tulku Rinpoche, Shadjin Lama of the Republic of Kalmyk (Russian Federation),

Co-Chairing the session on the second day, Ven. Geshe Jangchup Choeden, Abbot, Ganden Shartse Monastery, Karnataka, India, H.E Lyonpo Namgay Dorji, Minister of Finance, Kingdom of Bhutan, H.E Chuch Phoeurn, Secretary of State, Ministry of Culture and Fine Arts, Cambodia, among other distinguished speakers, discussed extensively on how to protect the environment and the Mother Earth from further onslaught.

In her valedictory address, Hon'ble Sushma Swaraj, Minister for External Affairs, Government of India, underlined the linkages between conflict and the environment. She also pointed out that while, on the one hand, a totalitarian approach where man is at the centre was propagated by a large number of Western philosophers, the Hindu and the Buddhist philosophers, on the other hand, remained deeply conscious of the need to preserve nature. The environmental degradation has reached an alarming stage today, and if corrective steps are not taken urgently, the future generations will not forgive us, Smt Sushma Swaraj cautioned the audience.

In his concluding remarks, General NC Vij, Director, VIF, stated that the conclave not only met all the objectives it had set out to achieve but even went beyond that. Scholars, heads of religious bodies, and other delegates who participated in the conference were aligned with the same thought process. The process initiated by the VIF would be taken further, General Vij assured the audience, while Mr. Masahiro Akiyama, President of the Tokyo Foundation, declared that Japan would host the next Hindu Buddhist Samvad (Dialogue) in January 2016. The Vote of Thanks was proposed by Most Ven. Lama Lobzang, Secretary General, IBC.

Global Initiative for Conflict Avoidance and Environmental Consciousness (Yangon 2017)

Dialogue for Peace, Harmony and Security

'SAMVAD' is an initiative of Vivekananda International Foundation (VIF) that was borne out of dialogue between the Indian Prime Minister Narendra Modi and Japanese Prime Minister Shinzo Abe. The purpose was to adopt principles of Asia's age-old spiritual teachings of Hinduism and Buddhism to address modern-day issues threatening human civilisation. It is imperative that inclusive and non-conflicting philosophies, exclusivist ideologies, spiritual masters and experts must engage in a frank, honest and all-encompassing dialogue on finding an alternative narrative and vision based on the spirit of understanding, acceptability, ethical behaviour, universal responsibility to shift the paradigm of global discourse on the two critical issues facing humankind: Conflict and Environmental Degradation.

Thanks to the collective efforts and invaluable contribution of our partners Sitagu International Buddhist Academy (SIBA), Yangon and Myanmar Institute of International and Strategic Studies (MISIS) and the presence of distinguished spiritual leaders from different faiths, keynote speakers, eminent scholars and panellists, and enthusiastic participants from about 30 countries, the SAMVAD-II, held in Yangon, Myanmar, on August 5-6, 2017 was a resounding success.

The highlight of the conference was a Round Table Summit of Spiritual Masters, in which the most eminent spiritual leaders of Buddhism, Hinduism, Islam, Christianity, Sikhism, and Jainism participated. The schedule included the inaugural session, Round Table Summit of Spiritual Masters, a Plenary Session and Academic Sessions on 'Evolving A Non-Conflicting Philosophical Paradigm for Conflict Avoidance, Peace & Harmony' on Day One, 'Environment Consciousness for A Sustainable World' on Day Two and a

Valedictory Session. Extensive deliberations over these two days established that Buddhists and Hindus must lead the initiative through a philosophical approach to the commonalities in their spiritual teachings to create a more tolerant, liberal and accommodative world that is based on mutual respect and acceptability of diversity of views to live in harmony with nature rather than seeing it as a resource to exploit.

Over 100 speakers addressed the gathering and presented their papers. The diversity of perspectives and views shared during presentations and deliberations indicated the openness and deep desire for a dialogue beyond the cliché and tokenism that most interfaith and peace initiatives have been reduced to. Despite different perspectives, all converged on finding a common ground for sustainable peace in a secured Mother Earth.

Venerable Dr Ashin Nyanissara, spiritual head and Chancellor of the Sitagu International Buddhist University (SIBU), in his opening address, set the tone for the conference by noting, *"The desire for peace exists everywhere, but most people are not able to enjoy peace, stability and security they desire"*. Video speeches of Prime Minister Narendra Modi and Prime Minster Shinzo Abe, speeches by HE the Governor of Uttar Pradesh, India, Shri Ram Naik, the Hon. Minister for Religious Affairs, Government of Myanmar, Mr Thura U Aung Ko, and the Inaugural Speech of HE the State Councilor Daw Aung San Suu Kyi read by National Security Advisor of Myanmar Mr U Theung Tun, set the ball rolling. The speeches underlined the emerging dangers to world peace and environmental catastrophe looming over Mother Earth, the only home for mankind.

In his video speech, Prime Minister Shri Narendra Modi referred to the critical questions about global challenges the world is facing today, like conflicts and climate change. He stressed that *"it is only through deep and prolonged dialogue – Samvad – that we may discover hidden synergies, resolving contradictions and the only way to cut through deep rooted religious stereotypes, prejudices that divide communities across the world and sow seeds of conflicts"*. He referred to the Hindu-Buddhist philosophical approach of living in harmony with nature, the need to revere nature and not just see it as a resource to exploit.

The Japanese Prime Minister Shinzo Abe, in his video message, referred to the Buddhist quote, *"May all beings be well and happy"*, to emphasise that the spirit of tolerance and compassion encompasses the coexistence of all lives. He warned that the spirit of tolerance was facing challenges today, and terrorism and violent extremism were expanding in trying to deny the existence of 'others' and painting our world in a single colour. He stressed that in Asia, *"we must let flowers of all different colours bloom in harmony."*

In her written speech, the State Counsellor and Union Minister for Foreign Affairs, Daw Aung San Suu Kyi, suggested that in tackling conflict avoidance, religious leaders of the world must impart the virtues of tolerance and non-violence as embedded in every world religion. She emphasised on making an attempt to establish community peace, regional peace and global peace. Her speech concluded with the call for:

- May the balanced mind make an unbalanced world balanced!
- May all conflicts and animosity be ceased!
- May peace and harmony prevail everywhere!

In his inaugural speech, the Governor of Uttar Pradesh, H.E. Shri Ram Naik, pointed to the great contribution of Hindu and Buddhist traditions to the modern world, such as yoga and mindful meditation. He noted that S N Goenka, a Burmese of Indian descent, introduced Vipassana (mindful) meditation to the world.

Among other notable speakers at the inaugural, academic and valedictory sessions were the Chief Minister of Yangon Region, U Phyo Min Thein, State Minister for Foreign Affairs of Japan, Nobuo Kishi, Hon Deputy Minister of Buddhasasana and Justice of Sri Lanka, HRSD Mitrapala, Minister for Social Affairs of the Government of Yangon Region, U Naing Ngan Linn, Deputy Chairman of the Parliamentary Ethical Sub-Committee and MP from Mongolia, Danzan Lundeejantsan and Ms Hiroko Tsuka, Executive Vice President of The Japan Foundation.

At the Plenary Session, Shri S. Gurumurthy from India and Professor Dr Khin Maung Nyunt from Myanmar set the agenda for the two days of deliberations to evolve a new paradigm of a philosophical approach to the two issues of Conflict and Environment that humankind is grappling with and the need for taking the initiative to the grassroots. They stressed on the need to break the shackles of ideologies and strive for philosophical debate as a means to develop universal understanding. Shri S. Gurumurthy emphasised on the need for introspection and review of scriptures and texts that steer religious ideologies towards intolerance and conflict. He cited reformist movements and debates within Hinduism that led to the discarding of texts and commentaries that sanctioned ills such as untouchability and Sati. Both stressed on the need for a people-participatory approach by going back to the fundamentals of our spiritual discourse of environment consciousness to shift from exploitation to respect and harmony with nature as co-habitants of Mother Earth.

Speakers at both the Round Table and the Academic Session, *'Evolving A Non-Conflicting Philosophical Paradigm for Conflict Avoidance, Peace & Harmony'* on Day One, stressed on the principle of freedom of practising one's religion without any interference from others. They noted that it becomes a major reason for strife only when certain radicalised elements try to force their own ideologies on others. The importance of dialogue and the capacity to listen to alternate viewpoints was emphasised. Speakers agreed that *Samvad* offers an opportunity to analyse the threats and challenges to world peace and suggests sustainable approaches such as the need for adopting non-conflicting ideologies. Eminent speakers such as the Hon. Minister for Religious Affairs, Myanmar, Mr Thura U Aung Ko and Mr Surin Pitsuwan, former Foreign Minister of Thailand and former DG, ASEAN, stressed the harmonious relations between religions for lasting peace and security.

The highlight of the Samvad II was the Round Table Summit of the Spiritual Masters on both Days 1 and 2. It was participated by the most eminent Spiritual Masters of Buddhism, Hinduism, Islam, Christianity and Jainism. The agenda for the summit included:

(a) Creating a conducive and compelling eco-system with the objective of emphasising the importance of dialogue and understanding for avoiding conflicts,
(b) Instituting a sustainable institutional model for frank and open dialogues between non-conflicting philosophies and ideologies and evolving a long-term perspective to promote institutions to carry forward ideas generated through these dialogues for lasting peace, harmony and security.
(c) Bringing environmental consciousness into global discourse and promoting significant changes in the way our present economic system is inherently structured on unsustainable conflict with nature.
(d) Establishing a global network of leaders in a wide range of social, political, environmental and intellectual arena, committed to the promotion of democratic values, conflict avoidance, environmental consciousness, universal responsibility and ethical behaviours

Referring to texts in "Abrahamic" scriptures that permeate exclusivist ideologies and lack of tolerance of other beliefs, several speakers cited how Hindus have rejected old Hindu scriptures and texts that do not fit into the 21st century. It was suggested that Muslims and Christians, too, may consider rejecting terms such as Kafir, Kufr and Heathen from their scriptures that may preach exclusivity and provide grounds for extremist ideologies. Several Buddhist masters, especially from Myanmar and Cambodia, referred to conversions as another cause of conflict, to which Hindu masters also empathised. Both stressed on respect for all religions and the spirit of coexistence. Muslim and Christian spiritual masters and scholars appreciated the concerns. They even agreed on the issues raised to put forth their perspectives and the need for continued dialogue where issues of mutual concern are frankly discussed. Muslim participants also spoke about a very critical phase that the Islamic world was passing through, with Muslims pitted against the rest of the world, horrendous killings by extremist ideologies in the name of Islam and sectarian conflicts. It was pointed out that there will always be people trying to hijack religion to suit their vested interests and hidden agendas. These elements would twist and turn the truths and translate them in line with their sinister plans, and they should not be looked upon as role models for any religion. It was stressed that truth is not just in books but must be experienced to be realised. Al-Haj Aye Lwin, Chief Convener of the Islamic Centre of Myanmar, while endorsing the spirit of Buddhist 'Kalama Sutra' (Buddha's sermon on free inquiry) and the Hindu sayings of Swami Ramakrishna, argued that any dialogue would certainly be counter-productive if anyone alleged that other religions are false or label the adherents of other religions as heathens or kafirs.

The Academic session on Day 2 was on the theme of Environmental Consciousness. The speakers concurred on environmental consciousness being the prime paradigm of socio-cultural cooperation and collective global action. Speakers also touched upon the philosophical underpinning of dharma. It was pointed out that the Earth is our only home in this universe, which we have taken for granted. Environmental protection would be possible only with self-awareness based on our ancient religious beliefs with respect to Mother Earth. It was noted that Hindu and Buddhist philosophies aver that man, being part of nature and not independent and certainly not its master, is fundamental to protecting and sustaining the environment and ecology. Hon. Minister of State for Home Affairs, Shri Kiren Rijiju, in his special address in the session on *Environment Consciousness for A Sustainable World* (Day 2), called for an urgent need to create a mass movement to create awareness on what crisis our planet and humans are facing and bring Environment Consciousness into the global political, religious, social and public discourse.

The highlight presentation in the Academic Session on the topic was by His Holiness Drikung Kyahgon Chetsang, from India and the supreme head of the 800-year-old Drikung order of Tibetan Buddhism. Referring to the Buddhist concept of interdependent origination that applies to everything in the world, he called for an authentic environmental consciousness to develop naturally once people recognise the deep interdependence between humans, plants, and animals. He stated that ancient Buddhist philosophy of interdependence is critical to the future of our planet. He also cited the "Go Green, Go Organic" campaign; his monastic order is developing in the Himalayan Ladakh region of India, where water supplies and the environment are under threat from global warming. He underlined that natural disasters and ecological problems do not choose people of one religion or nation. Speakers also quoted extensively from the Hindu philosophical perspective of revering nature and Mother Earth. Indian cultural traditions of 'Vriksha Vandana' (reverence of trees), 'Ganga Vandana' (worship of water) and 'Bhumi Vandana' (homage to earth) were also cited for inculcating environmental consciousness. Habitat loss, poaching and wanton killings by the meat industry for human consumption, which promote wastefulness and lack of compassion in society, were also spoken about.

The deliberations at the Round Table Summit of Spiritual Masters on Day 2 focused on evolving a consensus on an Action Plan and creating institutional means to take the Samvad initiative to the grassroots for dialogue among non-conflicting philosophical traditions and conflict-prone ideologies. Based on these, the Yangon Declaration was unanimously adopted. A copy of the Declaration is attached.

Hon. Chief Minister of Uttar Pradesh, Yogi Adityanath, was the Chief Guest at the Valedictory Session. In his address, he pointed out that Indian philosophies are not dogmatic and do not thrust their points of view on others. He made many references to Buddhist scriptures in his speech and stated, *"We have inherited this glorious tradition of tolerance and peaceful accommodation of ideas, differing from our own – something which has almost vanished in the contemporary world"*. Drawing parallels between Hinduism and Buddhism in their approach to sustainable development, he added, *"If the world must progress towards peace and prosperity, it is time to re-evaluate Lord Buddha and his Dhamma"*. His presence was highly praised, and his ideas resonated with the participants, especially among the Buddhist spiritual masters and other monks attending the session.

After the Conference concluded, delegates were taken to the majestic Shwedagon Pagoda, the religious symbol of Myanmar. The next day, Aug 7, they were taken on a day trip to the UNESCO World Heritage site of Bagan by a chartered flight courtesy of Sayadaw Dr. Ashin Nyanissara.

Conclusion

These two days have been immensely fulfilling for the VIF and its partners and hosts – the Sitagu International Buddhist Academy, Myanmar Institute of Strategic and International Studies, and The Japan Foundation. The Samvad aims to initiate intermingling and exchanges among religions, scholars, and institutions to build a new eco-system and take the initiative to the grassroots. The rich and scholarly discourse, research and frank opinions expressed by all the speakers, especially the spiritual masters, and unanimously agreed declaration give hope and guidance to steer us in this mission. The conference not only met the objectives set out to achieve but went beyond that. The proceedings and discussions in both the Round Table Summit and the Academic Sessions indicated an overwhelming consensus on finding an alternate narrative to issues and crises confronting human civilisation. All agreed on the urgent need to open a *'people-participatory paradigm'* over Conflict Avoidance and Environmental Consciousness at 'macro and micro levels', besides actions by governments multilateral and global bodies. This conference has given the lead to pursue that path. It also became evident that:

- The SAMVAD process needs to grow on a more formalised basis.
- The two religions may be able to lead the world in promoting sustainable models of conflict avoidance based on respect for all religions, philosophies, coexistence, understanding, and environmental consciousness so that humans and nature can live in interdependent harmony.

The Japan leg of the Conference will be held in Tokyo in January 2018, while the VIF is considering hosting Samvad III either in Sri Lanka, Nepal or New Delhi in 2018-2019. It is hoped that post-SAMVAD-II, this process of exchange and easy intermingling will gather momentum.

INDEX